Friends
Without
Benefits

WHAT TEENS NEED TO KNOW ABOUT A GREAT SEX LIFE

RON LUCE

A *TEEN MANIA* BOOK

Regal

From Gospel Light
Ventura, California, U.S.A.

Published by Regal
From Gospel Light
Ventura, California, U.S.A.
www.regalbooks.com
Printed in the U.S.A.

Library of Congress Cataloging-in-Publication Data
Luce, Ron.
Friends without benefits : what teens need to know about sex / Ron Luce.
p. cm.
Includes bibliographical references.
ISBN 978-0-8307-4717-7 (trade paper)
1. Chastity. 2. Christian teenagers—Sexual behavior.
3. Sexual abstinence—Religious aspects—Christianity. 4. Sex instruction
for teenagers—Religious aspects—Christianity. I. Title.
BV4647.C5L77 2010
241'.66—dc22
2010011337

4 5 6 7 8 9 10 11 12 13 14 15 / 15 14 13 12 11

Rights for publishing this book outside the U.S.A. or in non-English languages are
administered by Gospel Light Worldwide, an international not-for-profit ministry.
For additional information, please visit www.glww.org, email info@glww.org, or write
to Gospel Light Worldwide, 1957 Eastman Avenue, Ventura, CA 93003, U.S.A.

To order copies of this book and other Regal products in bulk quantities,
please contact us at 1-800-446-7735.

Contents

Introduction

Sex. It's the topic most parents seem to want to avoid at all costs, yet it's the topic that brought their kids into this world.

The intrigue of sex seems to know no age limit. The mystery of sex has provoked curiosity in the younger generation all around the world. The exposure of young eyes and ears to sexual content in music and movies has caused sex to become so commonplace that it forces us to ask the question, *Who knows the most about this?* Everybody seems to have his or her own opinion. Everybody wants to talk about it or express it. But the question is where to get our information about sex, which will lead to our sexual practices. The inventor of sex, God, had something great in mind when He first put it together, but today there are so many different opinions about sex that it's hard to truly understand His original intentions.

One of the most common beliefs about sex is that when it is practiced strictly among "platonic" friends, it is a harmless recreational activity. Hence, the term "friends with benefits" has become part of our common vernacular in the twenty-first century. In this book, you're going to read these and other people's opinions on sex. Some of the stories these people tell will be shocking, while some will be just funny. Through their eyes and experiences, you'll have the opportunity to protect yourself from the harm that they have inflicted upon themselves. Instead of just listening to what people around you are saying, what the media is telling you or "what everybody is doing," what you are about to read will open up your eyes to the real impact of these actions.

However alluring a music video or a movie might make sex look, we all know that they never show the consequences of what people who engage in sex outside of marriage have to endure. This might involve a sexually transmitted disease, or a broken heart, or an unwanted pregnancy, or a life filled with horrible memories. Through this book, you'll get a glimpse of what the inventor of sex originally intended when He thought it up. As a result, you'll have a shot at avoiding these pitfalls. If you apply the wisdom of what you read here, you'll have a chance of experiencing the rest of your life—the greatest ecstasy possible in your sex life—with the person whom you marry and commit to one day.

1

Friends with
So-called "Benefits"

In the last several years, it seems as though a rising trend among young people is to not get "emotionally entangled" in a relationship. As a result, they get wooed into "friendships" where they become involved sexually, thinking that this will prevent them from becoming emotionally entangled. What you are going to read in this chapter is a bunch of real-life stories from both guys and girls who have gone through this. From their stories, you'll see how it happened and how it turned out for them.

Some of these relationships are "open," meaning that those in the relationship know that the other person is having sex with lots of different people. Some are "secret," meaning they keep it just between them and their partner. Some of these couples are friends who get involved sexually but have no romantic relationship. They simply refer to the other person as their "hump buddy," while some call it a "booty call," and some even are so crass as to call it their "F–partner." Apparently, many teens don't see this as wrong, because they don't really know what a healthy dating relationship is supposed to look like. Because sex is so common in movies and music, it just seems like the normal thing to do.

Sometimes, "friends with benefits" or "hook-up buddies" will mean different things to different people. According to a *Teen Vogue* survey, 79 percent of respondents considered a hook-up as just kissing; 53 percent as touching; 46 percent as oral sex; and 47 percent as sex.[1] The question is, just how common are these types of relationships? How do they start? Why do they happen? And what are the real results? You are about to discover that the "benefits" of these types of friendships are not all they're cracked up to be.

Why Do People Do It?

You were a loser if you thought it was stupid.
You could get self-pleasure without having to commit to
a relationship with a boyfriend or girlfriend. You didn't
have to waste time to get to know a person. Then,
afterward, you could just be friends or acquaintances
again. No dating. No phone calls. No arguing.
No breaking up. No mess. It was simple and easy.

Most girls don't like to be seen
as having friends with benefits, but over
half of them have one.

I think friends with benefits
is a guy's excuse to get sex without
commitment, and all the while girls
are hoping they can trick the guy
into loving them. The sad thing is,
they wouldn't listen to truth if it
were told to them.

It's a cry for help and a "quick fix."
It doesn't fully satisfy; in fact, it never
really satisfies at all. We tend to want the
easiest and quickest solution, but food is
better when it's baked and not microwaved.
We can't submit ourselves to doing things
with those who have no morals, because
we know they don't care.

What I see is that girls just want to be
loved, so they give themselves up sexually to
a guy. All the guy wants from her is sex,
and he doesn't even care about her at all.

It makes people think that
sex is no big deal.

You think it will be easier because you can mess around with whomever and not have to stay with that person, but you also don't want that person to mess with anyone else. You run into jealousy, hurt and sometimes more loneliness. It is definitely a road I recommend no one go down.

How Common Is It?

Casual sex is becoming more and more common. For me, it was just a question of who or how many in a weekend. I remember hooking up with six guys in one night over the weekend. I would say that over 70 percent of my friends were sleeping with a different guy every two weeks, but saying that they were "just friends."

I thought, Oh, they are just friends, nothing will happen. After all, he plays bass in the praise band. Well, I came to find out she had been casually having sex with him, my ex-girlfriend, since she was 14. Not once had they dated. This guy killed me inside. He was a leader in our youth group and played in the church band. To them it was casual; to me it was sickening.

A woman at my church suggested
that a friend of mine should have a
friends-with-benefits relationship. When we
were shocked by this, she didn't understand.
She really didn't know what she was
suggesting and thought the phrase
simply meant having a close friendship.
I'm not sure adults are aware of what
being friends with benefits really entails.

I used to see it all the time back home,
even with people from my youth group.

In my school, and even in my church, everyone
had a person whom he or she was more
involved with than the rest. It wasn't a
commitment; it was more like security to them.

"Friends with benefits." I knew of people
who were "a couple," and a few days
later I would see them with someone
else. Only a few people I knew actually
stayed together, and even then a lot of
heartbreak came out of it.

Every single person I know has at least one
or more friends with benefits.

We need to be careful. Just because something is common—
whether it's in our church, our youth groups, our schools or our
Christian schools—it doesn't mean it's good for us. It doesn't mean
it's right or that we're not going to get hurt as a result. Junior-high
and senior-high schools are notorious for having a subculture
where so many ideas seem acceptable no matter how destructive
they might end up to be. The subculture can woo us and compel
us to do things that are absolutely going to destroy our lives.

How Does It Start?

We got closer and closer on the couch, and
then we were maintaining eye contact and
his arm was around the back of me. As the
conversation flowed, he eventually leaned in
and kissed me. I thought that was so cool,
because he was a friend of mine who "knew"
me. Even though I didn't have any makeup on
and I was in sweatpants, he still made me
feel beautiful by kissing me and showing
affection. So I felt like it was great,

especially when he started texting me every other night or every couple of days to see "what I was up to" (aka "wanna hook up?"). I loved the no-strings-attached relationship at the time because it was like I was in a relationship even though I wasn't. I felt really clever and dangerous when I began another "friends with benefits" relationship with another guy at the same time. I suddenly felt so coy, because I was using two guys at once and felt that I had the power.

I find too often that teens are becoming more and more afraid of commitment and getting their hearts broken, so they forego the relationship and go straight to the pleasing factors. I had a friend telling me that she was tired of the hurt she was continually going through, but she didn't want to give up the pleasure of the benefits that came with it.

I know of guys who have said to girls, "Can we be friends with benefits? Because I don't want my parents to know."

He would literally tell me the line, "I'm just not that into you." I thought after every time we hooked up it would be different! But it never was, and I knew that I would never be able to let go of him if it continued.

I had a friend, a "best" friend, and I slowly found out that he had started to like me. He started to get closer emotionally, even physically. We both got hurt and ended the "benefits," but our friendship wasn't the same anymore. We let sin mess it up.

He asked me to become his "cuddle buddy," even though he had a girlfriend. I was in shock. People don't think that it's as bad as having a one-night stand.

I think that our generation got caught up with just wanting to have sex, and this was the polite way to say, "I just want your body; the rest of you doesn't matter."

I was a friend with benefits. He convinced me that it was okay to kiss him, make out and get felt up and still be friends. There was oral sex involved on a few occasions. He convinced me in

*the moment that it was fine—
that I wouldn't get hurt—but all it
did was make a lot of secrets and push
me into a very dark place.*

Even in parents, the value of purity is gone.
My old girlfriend's parents believed that if you
were sexually compatible, you would have a
good marriage. Her dad encouraged me to
have sex with her because he considered me
a man of honor. If I were a real man of
honor, I wouldn't have given in. I would have
guarded her heart.

As you can see, many of these friends-with-benefits relationships start in a simple and casual way. The wise person would be on guard to make sure that he or she is not alone with the opposite sex so that these types of situations can't happen.

Why Do Girls Do It?

The boy doesn't want the responsibility of
caring for the girl's emotions, but he is
determined on using the emotions of the
girl to acquire physical intimacy whether
it is by kissing or sex.

When I asked her about why she did it and if she liked the guy, her answer was, "Josh? No way, never. I would never date him. He's a psycho!" I couldn't believe it. She would never date this guy, but it was perfectly fine in her mind to make out and more for hours on end. Her response? "It's no big deal." I was really impacted by her answer, because I thought that we as girls don't like to be used, but now girls use boys! Boys don't care if they are respected or not!

One particular girl I knew didn't have a father in her life. She would be "friends with benefits" with any guy who would be her friend. This happened with a lot of girls in high school. There are a couple I can think of, and the one constant in their lives were that they didn't have a father figure.

It's just a way to get what you want physically but not get so tied down emotionally. If you were in and out of relationships often, but were not being sexually active with them in any way, you could have a friend with benefits who you could always go to in between relationships to get that physical satisfaction you weren't getting.

Over time, I convinced myself that if I put up with the physical relationship, the person might someday grow to care about me more deeply. Instead, these relationships left me feeling confused and worthless. In my head, if I was worth someone caring about me, someone would have by now. I gave something I don't know if I can get back, and the only thing I received in return was shame.

Many girls would have sex with guys who were virgins, as a favor.

One summer, I had sex with two guys who I wasn't even in a relationship with. Because I did that, I now have spiritual ties with them, which I really regret. The temptation is so strong when you have experienced sex that you don't even care if you like the person; you just want to have the high you get when you do it.

Most of the girls, including myself, would want to have sex just for the sake of attention—to feel close to someone, to feel wanted by someone.

As you can see, what these girls were hoping for was not what they got. Most of them ended up feeling used and worthless. They had good intentions and hoped that the relationship would lead to something more, but that's obviously not what they got.

Why Do Guys Do It?

I had some friends who, if they broke up with their boyfriends or girlfriends, would go to this person and make out. One of the guys in my graduating class actually told me that he kept two girlfriends as "benefit girlfriends." He didn't have to be dating either one of them, and he usually wasn't. He just wanted to have two so he could have a back-up girl.

Many boys say that this is the only way they can be friends with girls. You have no commitment, because you are still getting all the goods. You will never buy the cow if the milk is free.

I had some friends in school who were girls
and didn't want to mess up the friendship
we had by getting into a relationship.
But we had sex at parties when we were
drunk, or high, or maybe just bored.

Friends with benefits force the two parties
into a strange, distorted commitment. I knew a
guy who had a girlfriend and also had other
"friends" with whom he was sexually active.
So he was basically asking these girls—if not
in word then in spirit—to be committed
to him even though he was not truly committed
to any one of them. Friends with benefits
are like concubines.

For me, "friends with benefits" was a pride thing—
a social acceptance thing. My friends and
I shot bragging rights at whoever could get the most
girls or mess around with the most girls without
getting caught. It was like a sport with rules
and rewards. It was mostly for pleasure, and
also for laughs, but it was really to bury our
mediocrity or loneliness and godless lives.

It appears that guys have found a new way to justify using the female gender: If they can somehow convince girls that they are just going to be "friends" and that they are not going to get emotionally attached, then they feel justified when they break up. They might say, "Hey, we decided to do 'friends with benefits,' and we agreed not to have any emotional strings attached, so *you* are in the wrong for getting your emotions involved." It's a clever line of reasoning that causes a huge amount of hurt. It really amounts to a new way for guys to justify acting like a predator, and so they can feel good about using a girl to get what they want.

What Is the End Result?

friends with benefits made me struggle emotionally and messed with my heart and mind and what I thought my worth was.

It's so glamorized, but it's really only fun for the guy. I completely fell in love with my friend, and when I found out he was doing the same with two other girls I knew, it broke my heart. The worst part is that even after that I kept it going. I convinced myself that if I were better or would let him do more to me (kinkier things) than the other girls, he would fall for me. It was one of the most painful relationships I've ever experienced.

My sister had a few no-commitment-but-with-benefits relationships, and it really destroyed her life. It made her feel worthless and ugly and like she was unlovable.
She has since strayed from her faith and is dating a non-Christian. Seeing her heart broken over and over by disgusting people who used my beautiful sister for their sick pleasure breaks my heart and infuriates me. These "friends" have almost played a home wrecker role, just as if a married person had an affair. Her respect for herself and her family went out the window completely.

When I ended it I felt used, and I knew that he was hurt. Our friendship was crushed. I gave all to get nothing back.

Eventually, almost always, one of the "friends" develops more than friendship feelings for the other person, and their "friendship" is never the same.

Our culture has moved from courting to dating to hook-ups and friends with benefits. Now that I am living for Christ, I realize how incredibly hollow I really was to do things like that, and how hollow I was after it was over.

A lot of the people in these relationships called each other "sex buddies." It seems like the girl would often mistake these for relationships. One girl I know allowed it in her life, and what happened to her would be what we would consider "rape." The guy believed he had free reign over her.

I have seen people as young as 12 who have or want "friends with benefits." I have seen those same people's hearts broken, their lives confused, and their bodies damaged because of what they've done. At school, it wasn't just that people were saying "everybody" was doing it; everybody truly was doing it. Their consciences were so deadened that they thought of is as nothing—just like eating ice cream. Yet when it was all said and done, hearts were broken and destroyed.

In the end, one of my old friends who was in a friends-with-benefits relationship felt empty, abandoned and ugly inside, like she was ashamed or something. Basically, friends with benefits make out or sleep with each other because they are already dating someone else or they want a "quickie."

The "users" in such an arrangement still want to have a sexual release, so they toy the guy or girl along with small acts of intimacy. The person gives the illusion of a relationship; however, no real relationship exists. The user never talks about it for fear that the used person will lose any hope of having a real relationship. This is a very selfish and destructive behavior for both parties. The user is being selfish, while the used person's perception of self-worth is totally being destroyed.

My friend Melanie, who is pregnant now, once said, "I heard he was good in bed, so I figured I'd get in on the action." Friends with benefits turns into a problem when one of the two turns the relationship into a commitment. The girl typically becomes hurt and possessive, starting arguments, while the guy gets jealous and controlling.

Friends with benefits is basically selling your body to the person who won't love you for who you are.

In the end, the pain and bondage are real. The person's heart is ripped for the adhesive we called a benefit.

One girl I know in a friends-with-benefits relationship had put up so many walls in her life from being hurt, and she never felt loved. She received attention and had so many boys in her life, but she didn't respect herself. She trapped herself in a dark hole. She wouldn't admit that she was in trouble even when help was offered.

My friend wanted to be loved by someone, but she knew deep down that she was his booty call, his doormat, something he could use. And in the end, she got very, very hurt by him.

These days, people have friends for whom they really have no feelings, but they mess around with each other anyway because they think it is okay and all they want to do is feel good. In reality, after you've been in such a situation you feel gross, and you try not to think about it because it's so gross. You keep doing it, but really it's one of the grossest feelings ever.

A friend tricked me into the whole friends-with-benefits thing, and I didn't even realize it until after it had ended. I thought of him as someone who was special to me, but he just thought of me as some kind of toy or game. I feel bad and guilty for going along with it and for thinking that I was falling in love with my best friend.

I had a friends-with-benefits relationship with one of those girls who just wanted sex, and that was it. It was a confusing time in my life, and I was deceived and let lust overcome my good sense. Before I knew it, we were having sexual relations. I thought everything was fine, but when I cut it off and got a girlfriend, I noticed that she was depressed all the time. When I looked at her bulletins on MySpace, I saw that she was brokenhearted and depressed—and all because of me. It made me stop dead in my tracks. It was then that I realized that I had become the type of guy I hated most of all. I was devastated. It took me over a year to forgive myself, even after she'd forgiven me.

I have to live knowing that I really messed up.
Although God has forgiven me, I will have to
tell my future husband what I've done.
It's a hard thing to think about, but I have
really learned from my mistake.

friends with benefits is a phenomenon that
occurs when two people in a relationship
are so insecure as people that they seek
refuge in each other without wanting the
world to know. I speak from experience.
There was a girl who I was attracted to
but was afraid to start an actual
relationship with because I knew I wasn't
responsible enough. While she was ready to
take the next step, her motives were wrong
as well, as she was a girl who validated
herself through relationships.

When you agree to be in a friends-with-benefits
relationship, you start to lose your friends, people talk
about you, you get worse friends that do the same thing,
and you look at yourself differently. You get heartbroken
when the person leaves and you feel alone, but you are

so used to having sex that you search out for it. It's a hard situation to get out of if you don't know God, because you do it so much and you're so used to it and you think about it so much. Friends with benefits hardens your heart and makes you hate the opposite sex, but you still go back to it. It's sin, and it takes you farther than you want to go.

When my friend got into a friends-with-benefits relationship, he stopped talking to me. About a month later he stopped doing things with that girl, but we still never talked after that. Friends with benefits not only tears the relationship of the girl and the guy, but also the guy and his friends.

As you can see, these friends with so-called "benefits" did not experience the benefits they thought they were going to get. Hopefully, by reading some of these stories you can avoid the pitfalls that they fell into. There is a lot you can learn about what sex is really supposed to be all about, which is what the rest of this book is about. In the next chapter, through the eyes of your peers, you will discover wisdom for the pitfalls to avoid and get a glimpse of how *great* God intended sex to be!

2

What Your Friends Say About Sex

What did they not say about sex . . .

(Female, age 19)

They hated it. It tore them apart physically and emotionally, and it has taken years for them to heal from their experiences.

(Female, age 19)

They said that if you do it you will become popular.

(Female, age 19)

They said sex was inevitable. I always assumed that high school was the best time to have sex.

(Female, age 16)

My friends said sex was okay and bragged like it was a "touchdown." There was a lot of pressure to do it.

(Female, age 17)

They told me to do it at least once so it wouldn't hurt on my wedding night, because that would stink. If you do it, you'll get good at it for your husband.

(Female, age 16)

I was told that if it was with someone that you really loved, then it was okay.

(Female, age 19)

It was accepted if you were dating.

(Female, age 18)

my friends said it was a normal part of being a teenager—fun, exciting, a thrill.

(Female, age 19)

I had friends who said they would wait until they were in love.

(Female, age 21)

Many friends said it was fun, though some cried to me because of the guilt they felt.

(Female, age 16)

You're cool if you do it.

(Female, age 16)

It was joked about a lot. Mostly the guys made perverted sex jokes. In high school I went to a Christian school, so it was always "honeymoon" jokes, but it was inappropriate.

(Female, age 19)

Some of my friends talked about oral sex and how it was not "real" sex. Their standard was to stop before having sex.

(Female, age 19)

They said it was fun and that I should do it even if I heard older people say I shouldn't . . . they don't like to have fun.

(Male, age 19)

I heard about how they can't wait to do it, how they were happy after they did it, and the different ways they did it.

(Male, age 19)

The more the merrier.

(Male, age 22)

my friends said it was normal to do
it when you were dating.

(Female, age 18)

They told me it was good and that
everyone was doing it.

(Female, age 22)

It seems like there are lots of different categories of friends. "Friends" can mean the people at school your age whom you just hear stuff from. Or it can mean the people you hang out with more often. Or it can mean the closest three to four people with whom you share the most intimate details of your life. Depending on which friends you listen to, you are going to hear different comments about sexual thoughts or activities. It seems that the more removed these friends are from you, the more bragging you will hear. The closer they are to you, the more details they will share about what they really think has happened to them.

The comments in this chapter are more like the ones you would hear from the friends who are the furthest removed from you. It's what you hear whispered around school. The problem is that if you hear it long enough, you start to believe it's true. However, as you will see in the upcoming chapters, if you listen to the heart of your closest friends, the reality about having sex is much different than the buzz around school makes it out to be.

What Our Culture Says About Sex

Our culture says a *lot* about sex. Everywhere you look there is a billboard, video, poster, movie or TV program telling us something about sex. Even the music industry encourages us to think about sex. Just look at the lyrics in some of today's popular songs:

I'm tryna put you to bed, bed, bed . . .

"Bed," by J. Holiday[1]

It's getting hot in here, so hot, so take off all your clothes.

"Hot in Here," by Nelly[2]

* * *

"Candy Shop," by 50 Cent

[We would like to quote from this song, but it's too vulgar to put in this book.]

I wanna sex you up . . .

Feels so right it can't be wrong.

"I Wanna Sex You Up," by Color Me Badd[3]

I want you to (rock the boat).

"Rock the Boat," by Aaliyah[4]

Let's make love, let's go somewhere,

they might discover us.

"P.D.A. (We Just Don't Care)," by John Legend[5]

Cause we off up in this jeep

We foggin' up the windows.

"Ignition," by R. Kelly[6]

Boy I'ma make you love me, make you want me . . .

Cause I don't want no one-minute man.

"One Minute Man," by Missy Elliott[7]

We ain't having sex,

We're making memories.

"This Ain't Sex," by Usher[8]

Sex Sells

According to Mediafamily.org, 22 percent of radio segments contain sexual content, with 20 percent of these considered "pretty explicit" or "very explicit." When there is sexual content on the radio, it tends to be during music segments (44 percent include sexual content) or during talk segments (30 percent). Almost half (44 percent) of sexual messages during talk segments refer to sex outside of pre-existing relationships, whereas less than 1 in 10 messages (6 percent) refer to sex within a pre-existing relationship.[9]

On average, a sexual scene occurs on TV 6.7 times per hour during the regular family viewing hours.[10] In fact, on MTV there are 3,000 sexual references each week.[11] Think about that: 3,000 messages a week telling us in subtle (and sometimes not-so-subtle) ways how we should think about sex and how we should be involved in it right now before we are married.

What is the impact of all these messages? According to the RAND Corporation, people who look at and listen to regular doses of these messages are twice as likely to get involved sexually before marriage. That means they are twice as likely to get their hearts broken, have unwanted pregnancies, and contract a sexually transmitted disease. They could even mess things up so that they are never able to have children. All this comes as a result of what they have seen in the media and how these messages have affected their lives.[12]

Consider some of the other findings that have appeared in recent news reports about the effects of all the sexual content in the media:

Dirty Song Lyrics Can Prompt Early Teen Sex:
Degrading Messages Influence Sexual Behavior,
Study Finds
ASSOCIATED PRESS, AUGUST 7, 2006[13]

BREAKING NEWS

Sexual Song Lyrics Linked to Early Sex
UNITED PRESS INTERNATIONAL,
FEBRUARY 24, 2009[14]

Media May Prompt Teen Sex
Teens Exposed to the Most Sexy Media Images
More Likely to Have Sex
CBS NEWS, APRIL 3, 2006[15]

Study Claims Sex on Television Contributes
to Teen Pregnancy
New Study Reveals that Sexual Content on Television
May Play a Role in Increased Rates of Teen Pregnancy
BUZZLE, NOVEMBER 3, 2008[16]

Britt Spooner, female bassist for Neon, stated the following about the way the media markets women in music:

> I usually do get comments about the way I look more often than my musical skills. . . . I think it is a lot harder and I don't think we've come much further in terms of feminism. Somehow the marketing of women is much more blatantly sexual than it ever was. In fact, being able to carry a tune and sing with musicians is the last thing that comes into it.[17]

What about some of the popular musicians and actors we see acting out these scenarios on TV—people like Britney Spears and Usher? What is happening with them? Take a look at some of these recent stories:

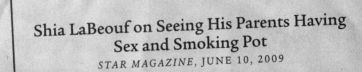

Shia LaBeouf on Seeing His Parents Having Sex and Smoking Pot
STAR MAGAZINE, JUNE 10, 2009

The actor—who supports his now-divorced parents—credits them for his sense of humor, saying: "My humor came from seeing my parents have sex, smoke weed, my mom being naked—just weird hippie stuff, twisted R-rated humor. . . .

"I have no answers to anything. None. Why am I an alcoholic? I haven't a damn clue! What is life about? I don't know. What I do know is, I screw up, and I know that I'm working on myself to be a better person. So I have no apologies. . . .

"I don't understand what it is I do that people want. I don't know what an actor does. I have no credentials. I don't know what I'm doing. To my mind, talent doesn't really exist . . . it's just a drive to be the best. I think acting is a con game."[18]

Pink Speaks Out About Split with Carey Hart
MTV NEWS, FEBRUARY 20, 2008

After two years of marriage, Pink and Carey Hart announced they were getting a divorce. Pink wrote about the split on her website: "The most important thing for you all to know is that Carey and I love each other so, so much. This breakup is not about cheating, anger, or fighting."[19]

Scoop: Lindsay's Drama Dooms Sam Reunion
SAN FRANCISCO EXAMINER, JUNE 18, 2009

"Sam let Lindsay back into her life as a friend, but now even a friendship seems impossible," the article reports a source told *People* magazine. "No matter how many times she promises to change, Lindsay loses control and starts acting like a maniac." The article continues, "This week also saw reports of LiLo partying hard and acting 'extremely oddly and erratically,' per another Page Six source. After a random encounter with a fellow clubgoer, she allegedly 'lost it and started yelling and cursing and flying around the room. She was not acting normal.' This does not sound like a happy life for Lindsay."[20]

Marilyn Manson and Dita Von Teese
SUNDAY TELEGRAPH, APRIL 22, 2007

In December of 2006, Dita ended the marriage after catching Manson cheating with a 19-year-old actress.

"I get the impression he thinks I was unsupportive," she says, "but the truth is I wasn't supportive of his lifestyle, and someone else came along who was." Manson's alcohol abuse and distant behavior were also cited as cause for the split. He is reportedly fighting for custody of the couple's three cats. A judgement of divorce was entered in Los Angeles Superior Court on December 27, 2007.[21]

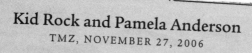

Kid Rock and Pamela Anderson
TMZ, NOVEMBER 27, 2006

They dated for years, but the marriage lasted only four months. Sources report that both Pam and Kid were in a race to get their papers filed first.[22]

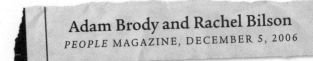

Adam Brody and Rachel Bilson
PEOPLE MAGAZINE, DECEMBER 5, 2006

Sometimes it's hard to separate reality from acting. These two dated onscreen on *The O.C.* and in real life, but the relationship did not last long.[23]

Reese Witherspoon and Ryan Phillippe
PEOPLE MAGAZINE, OCTOBER 30, 2006

"The biggest mistake," Phillippe said, "is not [working on my marriage], ignoring it and having the marriage fall apart because of laziness." Phillippe would not comment on reports that a relationship with his costar Abbie Cornish played a role in the demise of his marriage.[24]

BREAKING NEWS
Usher and Tameka Foster
THE INSIDER, JUNE 18, 2009

This rocky relationship ended quickly even though Tameka was pregnant with the couple's second baby. Usher now balances a fast-paced career and tries to make time to spend with his sons while still going through the divorce process. "What I do is, I try to get [my work] done and get home on the weekends if possible," Usher adds, "but when I'm with my boys it's just all about them."[25]

In a recent Kaiser Family Foundation study, 76 percent of teens said that one reason young people have sex is because TV shows and movies make it seem "normal" for teens.[26] The general message we receive from all of these reports is that people certainly can't be expected to control themselves. Sex is just what people do—particularly young people with raging hormones. So let's get this straight: We can train our dog not to go to the bathroom in the house, but we can't train ourselves? Are we actually saying that a dog is smarter than us? I don't think so.

The broader picture is that those in the media who produce content for teens (such as those at MTV) have a picture of what they want to make young people into.[27] For guys, this picture is a "mook"—a gross and immature perverted young adolescent. Somehow, they claim, acting this way will make you feel like a man. It is as if they are trying to train you to be a dog.

Ladies, they have a word for you, too: "midriff." They want you to act older than you are, strut what you have, and turn the guys' heads, as if somehow that will make you feel more important and valued. Yet, as you will see in the following stories that you are about to read, this is simply not the case. Once you have given away everything you can possible give away—your body, emotions, heart, purity, modesty—you will still feel empty and used by guys, used by the culture, and used by society.

The message we receive is that it is okay to have sex anywhere, with anyone, and at any time. Do it with anything that moves, and some things that don't. (Hmm . . . that sounds just like a dog.)

You would think that with all these messages floating around we would have a very happy culture. However, this is not the case. In fact, the data shows that people who sleep around and do what the culture tells them to do tend to be far less happy than those who have been married for several years and stayed true to having sex only with each other. We see more heartbreak, diseases and brokenness than ever before. You don't even have to look at the data—just look at all the stories, the tear-stained eyes of the families who have been broken up, and the romances that have been shattered after everybody has given to each other all the sexual intimacy they can possibly give. Whatever the culture is telling us, the answer is obvious: there must be a better way.

4

What Ignorant People Say About Sex

A lot of people say a lot of things about a lot of things.

Friends say a lot of things. Families say a lot of things. The culture says a lot of things. A lot of things we hear are just not true, but people call it truth.

We recently took a survey about all kinds of things that people are saying about sex. These are all total fallacies that, if nothing else, have great entertainment value . . .

Fallacy #1: Sex = Love

If a guy has sex with you, it means he loves you.

(Female, age 16)

It's okay if you are in love. You need to have sex to be "approved."

(Female, age 17)

It brings two people who aren't married closer together and improves their relationship.

(Male, age 19)

If sex truly equaled love, then prostitutes would be the happiest people in the world!

Fallacy #2:
You Need to See If You Are Sexually Compatible Before Marriage

You need to be sexually compatible before you get married.

(Male, age 19)

The more experience, the better.

(Female, age 17)

You need practice before marriage.

(Female, age 19)

It's better to have sex before you're married so you know what to do when you are married.

(Female, age 17)

The fact is that studies show that people who fool around before they are married (even if it is with each other) are actually less fulfilled in marriage and more likely to divorce. Believe me when I say that you will have no problem figuring sex out after you are married. Besides, if you don't get it just right, you can just keep trying again and again until you do!

Fallacy #3:
You Need to Have Sex to Be a "Real" Man

The more girls you can get to have sex with you, the more of a man you are. People who are "in love" just do that together.

(Male, age 19)

One way or another, you will always do it before you graduate high school. If you remain a virgin you will be more appealing to un-virgins, just so they can take it away.

(Male, age 19)

You need to have sex with a person before you marry them. You are not a man unless you've had it.

(Male, age 19)

This is just more of proving how much like a dog you are, not a man!

Fallacy #4:
Masturbation Is Okay

Masturbation is okay. (I heard this at school from a respected Christian!)
(Female, age 19)

I've been told that masturbation is okay.
(Female, age 18)

Masturbation is healthy.
(Male, age 21)

You have been given sexual passion in order to express your love in a passionate way to the one you marry. Any other way of releasing that sexual passion robs the person you will marry one day of that love. It belongs only to him or her. Practicing self-control in this area of your life will help you ensure that you will have an amazing sex life once you are married.

Fallacy #5:
Oral Sex Is Safe and Isn't Real "Sex"

oral sex isn't sex.
(Male, age16)

I've heard people say "oral sex isn't sex" or "condoms won't break for me!"
(Female, age 16)

If you have oral sex, you won't get a disease.
(Female, age 15)

Whether oral sex is "technically" sex or not, you are sharing a personal part of yourself with the other person—a part that should only be reserved for someone committed to you for the rest of your life. Oral sex is an expression of your sexual fantasy, and only the person you marry should ever have the privilege of ever experiencing that with you. In that sense, it represents something private that you would never really want anyone else to see.

According to a CDC report, 55.2 percent of males and 54.3 percent of females between the ages of 15 and 19 have engaged in oral sex.[1] Another study noted that out of the 75.3 percent of students who engaged in oral sex, only 2.9 percent used a condom or dental dam.[2] These people are taking a huge risk, because the idea that oral sex will in some way prevent you from getting a sexually transmitted disease is simply false. Here's what the research shows:

- Many STIs including gonorrhea, chlamydia, herpes, HPV and HIV can be transmitted by mouth-to-genital contact.[3]

- Research has proven that a virus which is contracted through oral sex can cause throat cancer. A study conducted by Johns Hopkins University has revealed that the HPV virus poses a greater risk in contracting cancer than smoking or alcohol.[4]

· HPV is the cause of roughly 70 percent of cervical cancers.[5]

Fallacy #6:
Condoms and Birth Control Prevent Pregnancies and/or STDS

It's fun, and you can't get pregnant or diseased the first time you do it (ha, ha).
(Female, age 17)

Condoms and birth control prevent pregnancy... even though there is still a risk.
(Female, age 17)

You can have safe sex with a condom.
(Female, age 16)

You can't get pregnant the first time. It's just practice for marriage.
(Male, age 19)

You can't get pregnant from doing it once.
(Female, age 21)

There's a very slim chance you'll get a disease
or pregnant if you use a condom.
(Female, age 16)

Condoms are 99 percent effective.
(Female, age 15)

It doesn't have an aftereffect.
(Female, age 19)

Regarding whether condoms ever break or not, the data suggests that if women use the male condom every time they have sexual intercourse and follow instructions every time, it is only 97 percent effective. This means for every 100 women who use the male condom all the time and always use it perfectly, there will still be 3 women who will become pregnant in a year. If women use a male condom but *do not* use it perfectly, it is only 86 percent effective. This means that for every 100 women who use the male condom, but do not use it perfectly every time, at least 14 women will become pregnant in a year.[6]

What about the claim that condoms prevent sexually transmitted diseases? Again, the data does not seem to support this conclusion:

- "If you always use condoms for vaginal sex, you will only reduce your chance of getting herpes by about half. To date, there is no evidence that condoms reduce your chance of getting herpes during oral or anal sex."[7]

· "Condoms provide no protection from HPV."[8]

· "Human papilloma virus differs from other STDs in its method of transmission; it is not spread from one person to another through the exchange of bodily fluids. Rather, it spreads through skin-to-skin contact. Since HPV is a regional, multicentric disease, it infects the entire genital area: the penis, scrotum, vulva and surrounding areas. Condoms do not cover the scrotum, nor most of the other areas that can be infected with the virus."[9]

· "The use of condoms, even if used properly every time, does not prevent chlamydia, as there is still skin contact around the genital organs, and the infection can spread through sweat and skin contact."[10]

Finally, there is absolutely no truth in the rumor that you can't get pregnant if you're having sex for the first time, as the following story from one girl proves:

I had sex when I was 12 years old. It was a weekend, and my parents were away. . . . Anyway, I was crazy about this guy named Darren who lived next door. We were classmates and next-door neighbors, but he did not know that I had a major crush on him.

So I invited him over that evening to watch some DVDs. We were in my room watching them, and then he asked me if I felt something about him. Things progressed, but I thought it was okay, because I had not yet started menstruating.

We got dressed when we were finished, and when my parents got back, it seemed to them like we were just watching television.

A month later, I started feeling nauseous and tired all the time. I didn't want to think I was pregnant, but I had no way of telling it from my menstruation, because I have not even had it yet.

One time when we were at my aunt's place, I saw a pregnancy test in their bathroom. I locked the bathroom door and took the test. It showed that I was *pregnant*.

At first my parents were angry and Darren didn't talk to me, but we finally decided to keep the child. Darren was told by his parents not to see me again, but we are trying to resolve the issue.[11]

Maybe you've heard your friends making these types of statements to you. Maybe you've even said it. But just because someone tries to pass off an urban legend as truth does not make it true. A lot of people end up with diseases because they believed some of these things that "sound right." They say, "Oh, everyone knows that. It's totally normal."

You don't need to be "normal." You are smarter than that.

5

What Kids Say About Sex

Kids can say the wildest (and most embarrassing) things, especially when it comes to sex and love. In this chapter, we'll look at some of the funny ways that kids have approached the topic. They probably had no idea how much their words would shock their parents!

A boy returning home on the first day of school asked his mom, "Mom, what is sex?" His mother believed in modern education and gave him a detailed explanation, covering all the bases of the tricky subject. When she finished the explanation, he produced an enrollment form he brought home from school and said, "Yes, but how am I going to get all that on this little square?"[1]

"Give me a sentence about a public servant," said the teacher. A little boy said, "The fireman came down the ladder pregnant." The teacher turned around to correct him.

"Don't you know what pregnant means?" she asked. "Sure," said the young boy proudly. "It means carrying a child."[2]

Several years ago I returned home from a trip just when a storm hit with crashing thunder and severe lightning. I came to my bedroom at 2 A.M. and found my two children with my wife. My wife, Karen, was apparently scared of the loud storm. I resigned myself to sleeping in the guest room that night.

The next day I told the children, "It's okay to sleep with mom when there is a storm like that, but when I am expected home, please don't sleep with mom that night." They said, "Okay."

After my next trip several weeks later, Karen and the kids picked me up at the terminal at the appointed time. Since the plane was late, everyone had to come into the terminal to wait for my plane to arrive along with hundreds of others. As I was entering the waiting room, my son saw me, came by and said, "Hi, Dad, I've got some good news."

I reached back and said loudly, "What is the good news?"

"Nobody slept with Mommy while you were away this time!" he shouted. The airport became very quiet.[3]

Little Mark was engrossed in a young couple hugging and kissing in a restaurant. Without taking his eyes off them, he asked, "Why is he whispering in her mouth?"[4]

A parent from my son, Carson's, school and I had to have a little intervention with their daughter and him. They were talking way too seriously about marriage and having kids for kids their age. The other mom did not think it was appropriate. I thought it was cute at first, but it did get a little obsessive for 5-year-olds. When finishing the conference, I wrapped up the conversation, "So what aren't we going to talk about anymore?" Carson exclaimed, "SEX!" really loudly. I turned beat red. The mom was really annoyed that my son used the "s" word in front of her daughter and asked how he knew the word. He replied, turning to me, "From the show you watch, *Sex and the City*." Needless to say, that was the end of our conference.[5]

One child, when asked how people fall in love, responded, "I think you're supposed to get shot with an arrow or something, but the rest of it isn't supposed to be so painful."[6]

One girl stated the following reason for why kissing was invented: "I know one reason kissing was created. It makes you feel warm all over, and they didn't always have electric heat or fireplaces or even stoves in their houses."[7]

Another boy, upon seeing a couple kissing, said, "He is trying to steal her chewing gum!"[8]

A 10-year-old boy gave this reason on what makes a successful relationship: "You've got to find somebody who likes the same stuff. Like if you like sports, she should like it that you like sports, and she should keep the chips and dip coming."[9]

Here are some titles of love ballads that kids came up with:

**"I Am in Love with You Most of the Time,
but Don't Bother Me When I'm with My Friends"**
(Bob, age 9)

**"How Do I Love Thee When You're
Always Picking Your Nose?"**
(Arnold, age 10)

**"Honey, I Got Your Curly Hair
and Your Nintendo on My Mind"**
(Sharon, age 9)

**"Hey, Baby, I Don't Like Girls,
but I'm Willing to Forget You Are One!"**
(Will, age 7)[10]

Five-year-old Christopher Walsh excitedly reported to his parents what he had learned in Sunday School. He told the story of Adam and Eve and how Eve was created from one of Adam's ribs. A few days later he told his mother, "My side hurts. I think I'm having a wife."[11]

Just reading these stories kind of makes you remember your innocence when you were younger, before you knew anything about these topics. It can also cause you to reflect on how perverse our culture has made love and sex. In fact, seeing the world through the eyes of a child is really not a bad idea—recovering our innocence, and then looking at it from that standpoint, could be exactly what we need.

What Animals Say About Sex

As we've seen, sex is everywhere. We see it all over our culture. We can barely flip on the TV, drive by a billboard, or surf the Internet without running into this obsession. But before our culture was as sexually obvious, it was raging in the trees, forests and oceans around the world. Yeah, that's right: Animals have been having sex for centuries. In looking at the animal kingdom a bit more closely, we can discover some of the most unique sexual habits among our co-inhabitors of this great earth. In this chapter, we'll see what we can learn from observing a number of species of animals.

Lions

 Male lions get a whole "pride" of wives. If a stronger male comes and defeats him, then all of the wives belong to the champion. During a mating bout—which can last several days—male and female lions will have sex from 20 to 40 times a day, and they are likely to forgo eating during this time.[1]

Hippos

For hippos, it's all about how good the males smell. Once they have staked out where they want to pick up their mate, they make a concoction of urine and feces. After this irristible scent starts to spread, the male hippo increases its range by twisting his tail like a propeller. Female hippos nearby just can't stay away and drift into the marked territory, where the two play in the water and then mate.[2]

White-footed Parrots

These are the only animals that include kissing in their mating ritual. To choose a partner, the birds lock beaks and gently French kiss each other. If all goes well, the male shows he is ready for more by throwing up his food for the female. After mating, both share parenting responsibilities.[3]

Penguins

Some animals take commitment more seriously than others. Many species of penguins have only one partner in their life. When penguins choose a mate, the two stand facing each other with their heads back and belt out a loud song declaring their commitment to each other while trembling. When they have been together for a few weeks, the male lays his head on the females mid-section as a signal that he is ready to mate, and the two disappear for a short while—the mating process is three minutes max. For emperor penguins, neither will mate again for a year.[4] Both share responsibilities for preparing for and tending the young.[5]

Sea Lions

Young sea lions are obsessive observers of the older generation's mating process. They watch their elders yearly, and by the time they are of age, they have it down pat. Males often stop eating for days to fully devote themselves to mating, staying in their territory and mating with an average of 16 females.[6] Some male sea lions have actually been known to "mate themselves to death."[7]

Dolphins

Dolphins seem to enjoy reproduction more than other animals, mating up to several times during a day. However, don't be too impressed with their stamina—each mating session lasts 12 seconds at the most.[8]

Octopi

For an octopus, sex is all about keeping the species moving forward. The male's and female's sexual organs don't even connect during the process. After it's over, the male will move his sperm with his tentacle to the female. The female will stop eating, placing all of her focus on the survival of the eggs. After the eggs hatch, she dies. Her job is done.[9]

Galapagos Tortoise

When two male Galapagos tortoises meet, especially at mating time, they will rise up on their legs and stretch out their necks to assess which is dominant. The shorter male will leave, and the winner will proceed to find a mate. When he has found her, he will ram the female and nip her legs until she draws them in, thereby immobilizing her. He proceeds. Mating can last for hours, during which time the male grunts and yells loudly. If he seems terribly excited about the whole deal, it's because he has been waiting a long time—it takes 40 years for the Galapagos giant tortoise to reach maturity.[10]

Grasshoppers

Grasshoppers are serious about wooing their female companions. Male grasshoppers have around 400 songs they sing to catch the female's attention. Even more amazing is that each song has a different meaning. There's one for "I'm flirting with you," another for "let's get together," and another for "it's time for us to make baby grasshoppers."[11]

Lynx Spider

For the male lynx spider, forget about the songs or sweet smells—sex is just a way of life. When he's ready to mate, he will capture his mate in his web and wrap her up. He'll allow her to move around enough in the web to see some of the food he's caught for her. Then, while she is feasting on bugs, he will get on top of her and complete the mating process.[12]

Praying Mantis

For praying mantises, the mating process goes something like this:

Male: Hey, I'm Joe. So, what's your name?
Female: My name is Sally.
Male: Want to get together?
Female: Sure!
Male: Wow, Sally, I'm so gla—
Female: [Chomp!] Hmm, tastes like beef.

So much for special treatment—the female praying mantis often beheads her partner during mating.[13]

As you can see, all of these different species have a wide variety of sexual practices. Essentially, they are just following their instincts—something that was put inside of them as to what they should do in order to reproduce.

For example, let's say Fido goes and has sex with FiFi, her sister, her mother and her daughter. He will not feel bad about this, get arrested, get a disease or break anyone's heart by doing this. Why? Fido is a dog. He has no moral code inside of him. He has no sense of right or wrong. He just does what his instinct tells him to do.

We have a lot of guys in our society who act a lot like Fido. They claim to be just "following their instincts," and they use this as an excuse to treat women like garbage and fool around as many times as they want with as many people as they want. Following instincts is what animals were designed to do and, as a result, they continue their species. But we human beings are not just overgrown animals. If we run our lives by "instinct" and do whatever we want to do, we will just get ourselves into trouble.

You and I have a moral code written on the inside of us that God put there. Even if we don't believe in God, it's still there. When we violate that moral code, bad things happen to us. If we act like Fido, we might end up with a disease, children that don't have a parent, break another person's heart and destroy our reputation. We were not meant to run our life by instinct but by *wisdom*. Wisdom is doing the right thing even when our instinct desires something different.

As you've seen in this chapter, animals have a wide variety of practices when it comes to mating because God put different instincts in them. But He also gave you and me a different class. Sex for humans is designed to be much more than for reproduction.

7

What Parents Say About Sex

"   "

(Moms)

"   "

(Dads)

Nothing.

That's right . . . nothing. Most parents don't say anything to their kids about sex. They feel awkward about approaching the topic, and this makes their kids feel awkward. In the process, not much of anything is communicated, and even when something is communicated, the information is less than helpful.

I am reminded of one 15-year-old boy who told me that the sex talk he received from his parents went something like this: He saw one dog humping another in the kitchen and asked his mom, "Mom, is that what sex is like?" His mom said, "Yeah, pretty much." That was the entire sex talk.

In this chapter, we will look at what some teens have said their parents told them about sex, and what they wished their parents had told them.

What Teens Say Their Parents Told Them About Sex

It's an awkward subject, but mom did a pretty good job. I was kind of weirded out at first, but I have known that it is a precious gift from God to give your spouse.

(Gender and age unknown)

My mother gave me the old-fashioned birds-and-the-bees talk. She told me I was healthy enough to get pregnant.

(Female, age unknown)

They told me, "Save sex for marriage."
They told me it was a treasure and that I
needed to guard it with all my heart.
(Female, age 17)

My parents did not talk to me a lot about sex
because it seemed like they thought the less I
knew the better off I would be.
(Gender and age unknown)

It was a while ago... I guess it was kind of
awkward. Now it would be easier to talk about.
(Female, age 16)

They sat me down and told me why not to
do it. I mostly learned things when I
was at youth group or reading the Bible. I mean,
it's not hard to see. It's all over God's Word
because it's so important.
(Female, age 15)

My mom seemed very nervous, like I should
be telling her. But I think if I were in that
situation, I would have been nervous too. I
just told her that I knew, and she told me
things she figured out on her own.
(Female, age 16)

Mostly my mom talked to me about relationships and sex. She did warn me to watch out for any creepy guys who might try to pull something.

(Female, age 16)

I'd say they made it clear that sex was only for reproduction, and that it's only okay after marriage. I wish they would have told me how it destroys people's lives and futures or given me an effective way to say no to make a guy get it right away.

(Female, age 16)

The only time my mom explained anything about sex was when I started my period. She explained why it was happening, but she didn't go into details, because I was 10.

(Female, age 16)

Many times the subject was avoided.

(Female, age 20)

My parents did not want me to be surprised when I heard about sex at school.

(Female, age 17)

They were pretty vague.

(Female, age 15)

They did a pretty good job and it didn't disturb me or my sister too bad. LOL.
(Female, age 15)

They gave me good information. Some of it was indirect, but I picked it up.
(Female, age 17)

We had multiple talks about it.
They were more serious.
(Male, age 16)

They talked about how the Bible says sex was a gift from God for marriage.
(Female, age 16)

They were nervous and did not think I knew this stuff. They didn't go deep.
(Male, age 17)

They gave me their honest opinions and thoughts and everything.
(Female, age 15)

They told me to wait until marriage.
(Female, age 21)

They talked about how to stay pure.
(Male, age 19)

They said sex creates a tight emotional bond between two peoples' hearts that, outside of marriage, causes an immense amount of emotional pain when you break up.

(Male, age 19)

They spoke about purity and why it's important, and that I'm worthy.

(Female, age 18)

They wouldn't have told me anything. We had a very awkward household. There was no dad in the picture.

(Male, age 23)

They said sex is something beautiful and not disgusting.

(Female, age 17)

What Teens Wish Their Parents Had Told Them About Sex

I think I would have liked to hear my mom talk about some of the things in her past. I would have liked to have been given the emotional part of it.

(Female, age 16)

I would have rather found out from them than the media.
(Age and gender unknown)

My dad just stared at me and Mom was real preachy about it. I wish they would have just made it more casual.
(Male, age 19)

My parents never really had "the talk" with me. I guess they figured I wouldn't have sex. I wish they would have mentioned the regret and agonizing pain of it.
(Female, age 16)

My parents never really talked to me about sex, but then I don't know if I would have wanted them to. I learned about abstinence through them, and that was good. I wish they would have told me that not everyone supports abstinence and that I will be constantly surrounded by people who are having sex when I'm older.
(Female, age 16)

The struggles were not addressed. I wish my parents would have told me how hard it is to remain pure. I wish they would have told me how they overcame their own temptations at my age or how they failed.
(Female, age 17)

We never really talked about it.
My mom gave me and my sister books on
the Christian perspective about premarital
sex, and that was it.

(Female, age 18)

I wish they would have told me how
easy it is to slip and go from making out to
losing your virginity. No one ever explained
to me how fast and crazy it can be with
all your hormones going.

(Female, age 16)

There was no talk. I wish I would have
known the importance of purity.

(Female, age 17)

I wish they would have told me how important it is
to keep my virginity. It brings shame and guilt,
and sex should be saved for marriage.

(Female, age 18)

My parents were never up to talking about
sex. I wish my mom would have been more
open with me about her past relationships.

(Female, age 18)

They explained to me why I need to stay pure and how to stay pure. I wish they had told me more about how hard it is to not have sexual thoughts.

(Male, age 17)

The talk was not as good as I would have liked. I learned way more at my class at school than at home. I wish my parents had said more what it is. I would have liked to have a healthy understanding of sex so I knew the dangers about it.

(Male, age 16)

They talked about physical purity, but it was not concrete enough for me to develop boundaries or guard my heart. I wish they would have told me how sex is attached to emotions.

(Female, age 16)

I wish they would have told me how beautiful it is to wait and helped me understand that better.

(Female, age 16)

We did not really talk about it much. I wish they would have said what a trap sex would be.

(Male, age 20)

My parents just told me not to
have sex. It was not really a conversation.
I wish they would have told me that
it has consequences.

(Female, age 15)

I wish they would have been more open and
honest about leading me to purity. I wish they
would have given me more answers and more
of a Christian perspective.

(Male, age 19)

I wish they would have started talking to me
about it at a younger age. I wish they would have
been the first to reveal some of those things to
me and also show biblically why to stay pure.

(Male, age 19)

I wish they would have talked
about it more.

(Male, age 19)

I wish they would have sat down and talked with me
instead of giving me a book.

(Female, age 19)

I wish they would have talked to me about it.

(Female, age 18)

I wish they would have been more open about it. Not that they had to have every detail, but I shouldn't have had to find out as much as I did from the Internet.

(Male, age 20)

I wish they would have had one-on-one conversations with me where they found out what was really going on.

(Female, age 19)

I wish that they would have just told me.

(Female, age 18)

I wish they would have taught me about sex.

(Female, age 19)

I would have liked to have them tell me how to keep my thoughts pure and guard my emotions.

(Female, age 19)

I would have liked them to talk about the true heart behind why I should wait.

(Female, age 19)

They could have told me that pornography is evil.

(Male, age 19)

I would have liked to have heard how sex tears the soul. I wish my dad would have given me more insight about his teenage years and girls in general.

(Male, age 18)

If they had talked to me about sex, I would have wanted them to tell me that I should wait for the person I am going to marry.

(Male, age 21)

I wish they would have been more open and told me more about how bad they felt when they didn't stay pure for each other.

(Female, age 16)

I wish they could have told me more about what God says about it.

(Female, age 19)

I wish my parents had told me something so that when we learned about it in school I wasn't the only clueless one.

(Female, age 16)

I wish at a younger age they would have really explained to me how precious sex is.

(Female, age 16)

I would have liked to have heard stuff about what an orgasm is, because I had to find that out from my friends.

(Female, age 16)

I wish my dad would have talked to me about it. One time I heard something on the radio about dads taking their daughters out on dates to model what it should be like, and I thought that was a really great idea for both parties.

(Female, age 20)

They could have told me that staying pure doesn't just mean you don't have sex; it means you don't do anything that you know you wouldn't want God to see. That includes your thoughts, because He does see it all, and it starts in your mind.

(Female, age 15)

I wish they would have said that it's normal to have those feelings and to want to have sex. Otherwise, it's not regarded as something priceless.

(Female, age 16)

I wish they had told me "why not" instead of "do not."

(Female, age 20)

*I wish they would have talked to me
more about relationships and boundaries.*
(Female, age 21)

They could have told me how it affects
you emotionally.
(Female, age 16)

I wish they had told me how it
makes you feel afterward—unworthy—
and the value of purity.
(Female, age 24)

I would have liked to have
heard about the side effects and the
emotional pain sex causes if you do
it before marriage.
(Male, age 19)

I wish they would have told me earlier.
They started talking about it when I was
9 or 10, but by that time I already had a
perverted view of it.
(Female, age 19)

They should have told me not to do it.
(Male, age 22)

They could have been more open about the things they struggled with and the things I would face. Also, I wish they had not been afraid to talk about the awkward things, like oral sex, homosexuality, masturbation, and so forth—the different things teens struggle with.

(Female, age 19)

I wish they would have explained about masturbation.

(Female, age 19)

I would have liked to have them tell me about the consequences of sex and God's Plan.

(Female, age 22)

I wish they would have had one-on-one conversations with me where they found out what was really going on.

(Female, age 19)

I would have liked them to tell me how it creates a tight emotional bond between two people's hearts that, when done outside of marriage, causes an immense amount of emotional pain when you break up.

(Male, age 19)

They could have told me more details
about the emotional attachment
involved with masturbation and oral sex,
and why it's wrong.

(Female, age 19)

I wish they had told me God's advice and
view on it and why purity is so important.

(Female, age 20)

They could have talked more about it. I'm still
confused by some emotional stuff, but I now
know how to go about a godly relationship. My
parents will talk now, though.

(Male, age 19)

I wish they would have been educated on what
true emotional/physical purity is, how to communicate
what sex is, and the need for godly relationships.
I wish they would have known about masturbation
being wrong or communicated that to me.

(Female, age 18)

They should have told me about the different
temptations and how to overcome them. I
was really unprepared for high school.

(Male, age 19)

I wish they would've sat down with me and actually talked about it, now that I've had to experience so much.

(Male, age 20)

Parents' attitudes about sex seem to range from telling their kids nothing to threatening them with death if they ever do anything to handing out condoms and saying, "By the way, it's okay if you want to go and get on the pill." If parents are not going to teach their kids what is proper and what the best use of their bodies is, where are they going to learn?

When our kids were young and began to ask where babies came from, my wife, Katie, and I gave mild answers. As they got older, they were ready to understand more and more. My wife and I always tried to have a loving marriage and treat each other openly with love and respect and, when they were the right age, we told our kids that we loved each other so much that we made a baby, and they came out. That formed the right picture in their mind of what sexual intimacy is all about.

Many parents are afraid to talk about sex because they blew it when they were young and don't want to tell their kids the truth about their own background. Some parents are afraid to share about their past with their children because they worry it will send a message that it's okay for them to follow in their footsteps.

Although it may be gross to imagine your parents being involved sexually, you know it happened, or you would not be here! However, as you've seen in this chapter, not all parents know how to communicate to their kids the wise use of their body, even when it's raging with hormones. Maybe that is why you are reading this book—you, too, are curious about sex and how you can have great sex for your whole life. If so, keep reading!

8

What Experienced Teens Say About Sex

What you are about to read are stories from guys and girls told to you as if they were your closest friends. Imagine sitting across from your best friend as he or she tells you about his or her sexual situation. You would be hearing not just how and what happened, but *how they felt* afterward. Many of these guys and girls, as you will see, are ringing with regret. Listen to their stories carefully and try to see life through their eyes. Feel their heart as you listen to their stories.

How old were you the first time you had sex?

14 (female)

What was the situation?

I was with two guys in a truck outside my house. They were both pressuring me to have sex. I continually kept saying "no" or "I don't know," but I finally gave in because I thought they wouldn't like me. I lost my virginity to two guys on the same night. It was my first night for everything.

What did you go through emotionally?
I went through guilt. I do regret doing it.

....

How old were you?
17 (female)

What was the situation?
I'd fooled around with a couple of guys, but I hadn't actually had sex. There was a guy who I had a big crush on, and he wanted to sneak over to my house in the middle of the night. We made a regular habit of this, and I did everything with him except actually have sex. One night, he decided he wasn't going to listen to me. I kept telling him no, but he did it anyway.

What did you go through emotionally?
Emotionally I had some big problems. I hated myself and felt like I wasn't good for anything. I felt like a whore, even though what happened wasn't my fault. I've torn myself apart by doing things with him and other guys. I'm heartbroken.

How old were you?

15 (female)

What was the situation?

I got used by a guy. He and I don't talk anymore. I only did it because I thought it would change the way he felt about me and make him actually like me.

What did you go through emotionally?

I went through depression, regret and sorrow. I regretted ever thinking about doing anything with him. And, to this day, I still wish I hadn't done anything.

How old were you?

16 (female)

What was the situation?

I haven't had sex, but I'd say I've lost my purity.

What did you go through emotionally?

Very much regret. I felt like a slut, a tramp.

How old were you?
16 (female)

What was the situation?
I was pressured into it from a guy I thought I really liked. Then afterward he wanted to break up when I didn't want to mess around anymore.

What did you go through emotionally?
It was definitely hard, like a slap in the face. I felt lost and broken, and I was too embarrassed to talk about it to anyone. I completely regretted it.

How old were you?
16 (female)

What was the situation?
I had oral sex.

What did you go through emotionally?
I felt guilty at myself, and I felt like part of my childhood was gone.

How old were you?

16 (female)

What was the situation?

The first time just started with a kiss. After I kissed him, he told me he would never try to take my purity, but I was thinking, "Hey, you are right now," and then we ended going a lot further.

What did you go through emotionally?

Even when I was kissing him, I knew he wasn't the one. And I wanted so badly for him just to hold me and love me, and not expect anything.

....

How old were you?

17 (female)

What was the situation?

The first time I slept with a guy was because of a horrible decision I made based on being left alone by a previous boyfriend. When I say "left" I really mean it—he left without even saying "it's over" or "goodbye." The guy I slept with was a friend whom I found refuge in, and because we were just friends, I felt safe that he would not abandon me.

What did you go through emotionally?

After having sex for the first time, at the moment I felt glad that I had done it, because I felt satisfied. But when I went to church the next weekend, my mistake was staring me in the face. I suffered a lot after my bad choices. I always felt guilty, and sex was never satisfying.

How old were you?

There's been a couple of times—12 and 16 (female)

What was the situation?

When I was 12 I was babysitting with a family friend who I referred to as my "cousin." He was two years older than me, and I was curious.

What did you go through emotionally?

I felt bad, but I didn't know why, so I told my mom. Yeah, I regret it, because I sort of lost her trust.

How old were you?

15 or 16 (female)

What did you go through emotionally?

I felt nasty, like trash, after the first time it happened. I ran to my best friend's house at 4:00 in the morning crying. I felt dirty, like damaged goods, but it was nothing compared to the rape.

How old were you?

15 (male)

What was the situation?

I was dating a girl who went to my church, and it happened at my house.

What did you go through emotionally?

I felt uncomfortable after the affair, because she was 18.

How old were you?

17 (female)

What was the situation?

I snuck my boyfriend into my bedroom at night, and then it just happened.

What did you go through emotionally?

Regret. I still have trouble forgiving myself.

How old were you?

Sadly, I was only 12 (female)

What was the situation?

I was with a boy who told me he loved me, and I believed him.

What did you go through emotionally?

I didn't feel like a child anymore, and I was disgusted with myself.

....

How old were you?

12 (female)

What was the situation?

I was going out with this guy who was 16-almost 17-and he pressured me into it.

What did you go through emotionally?

I was completely changed, and I regret it with all my heart. I wish I could take it back.

....

How old were you?

Almost 15 (female)

What was the situation?

I was with this guy I liked, and he was really into worldly things.

What did you go through emotionally?

I went through a really hard time afterward. I regretted it a lot.

How old were you?

15 (female)

What was the situation?

I was forced into it by a boyfriend.

What did you go through emotionally?

I felt pretty dirty, I mean, I felt low.

....

How old were you?

14 (female)

What was the situation?

I started dating this guy who was 23 whom I had met through a friend. He gradually led me into kissing and more physical things, and then one night I gave in after many make-out sessions and gave away my virginity.

What did you go through emotionally?

I regretted it so much—more than anyone can know. He said he loved me, and I was confused. But he didn't love me, and he broke my heart.

How old were you?

15 (female)

What was the situation?

It was not sex, but oral sex with my boyfriend.

What did you go through emotionally?

I cried and regretted it and tried to change.

....

How old were you?

14 (male)

What was the situation?

I was at a party and me and this girl started flirting, and one
thing led to another and... yeah.

What did you go through emotionally?

I was excited at the time, but regret came later when
I got saved.

....

How old were you?

15 (female)

What was the situation?

I was at a boy's house after homecoming. We were
the only ones home.

What did you go through emotionally?

I mostly felt the loss of innocence and regret because my future husband wouldn't have me first.

How old were you?

11 when I started messing around; 14 when I lost my purity (female)

What was the situation?

I was in a relationship with a 17-year-old. We were both Christians and we tried to stay pure, but we kept putting ourselves in bad situations. He graduated high school and had come to live with my family. At night I would go and lie next to him and fall asleep . . . and we let our emotions go crazy. He was gentle with me, but it started really hard sexual bonds in both our lives.

What did you go through emotionally?

I felt as if I failed, so I just kept messing around with guys. I felt like every guy was going to treat me the same way, and for the most part they did. I lived a lie from my parents, and it was emotionally hard because I needed my mom. God was continually convicting me, but I didn't know how to get free from this trap.

How old were you?

14 (female)

What was the situation?

I was at a high school party and was dancing with this guy who enjoyed my presence. As we were dancing, he pulled me over to this chair and began to grope me, and then one thing led to another.

What did you go through emotionally?

It was one of the hardest things, because he moved away at the end of the summer and never called or kept in any kind of contact with me. I felt used, unworthy and broken.

......

How old were you?

16 (female)

What was the situation?

I have not lost my sexual purity, but with my first boyfriend my friends and his parents encouraged us to move quickly. We played with one another's emotions.

What did you go through emotionally?

Much regret. I felt disgusted and gross!

How old were you?

16 (female)

What did you go through emotionally?

I felt so dirty and unworthy. I cried so much, because I knew I had disappointed my parents and had given in to my stupid culture that said, "They will love you more if you do it." I regret it so much.

....

How old were you?

16 (male)

What was the situation?

It started with what seemed like innocent kissing, but escalated very quickly. The setting was a dark room with no one around—a dangerous setting to be in.

What did you go through emotionally?

A ton of sadness and depression. I felt very alone, even with many people around.

....

How old were you?

17 (female)

What was the situation?

My boyfriend spent the night at my house, and I snuck out of my room to join him on the couch.

What did you go through emotionally?

I was shocked at my own behavior, and it started a
cycle that was hard to break.

....

How old were you?

14 (female)

What was the situation?

My brother had a friend over and so did I; we just all
looked up when my parents were sleeping.

What did you go through emotionally?

When I was younger I thought it was cool, but as I
continued looking up as I got older I felt serious regret.

....

How old were you?

16 (female)

What was the situation?

It was on a dare, and I didn't want to be
a chicken.

What did you go through emotionally?

I now regret everything I did. I didn't feel like
I was loved unless I slept with guys.

How old were you?
16 (female)

What was the situation?
I was caught by the cops in my parents' van in a park.

What did you go through emotionally?
I was kicked out of my parents' house for a time. Despair. Regret. Guilt. Frustration. Constant tears.

....

How old were you?
15 (male)

What was the situation?
I was riding in the back seat of a car with a girl, and stuff happened.

What did you go through emotionally?
Even now I regret what happened. Every time I see her, it comes back.

....

How old were you?
16 (female)

What was the situation?
I was going out with a guy for months, and we both wanted to stay pure. One night we went

to a party together and left early. We ended
up having sex in the back seat of the car.

What did you go through emotionally?

I was so angry at myself. I regret it
completely.

Here are some other comments from teens about what they
felt after having sex for the first time:

I was an emotional wreck.
(Female, age 19)

I thought I loved her and she loved me, but
that wasn't the case. I regret all of it!
(Male, age 19)

I didn't regret it until we broke up, and
then I felt shame and deep regret. I
thought it was forever, but I was just
naive about the whole situation.
(Female, age 19)

I felt disgusted, stupid, trapped, ugly—
like I was a plaything.
(Female, age 19)

It is said that wisdom comes from learning from the mistakes of others. All of us can say, "I sure learned from that mis-

take." How much better would it be if we could learn from others' mistakes so we do not actually have to live through those pitfalls! Read between the lines of these stories, and you will see wisdom. The wisdom of their experiences is the same wisdom spoken of in the Bible.

9

What Virgins Say About Sex

You might think, *What would virgins have to say about sex?* In fact, they have a lot more to say than you might expect. In this chapter, we asked a number of virgins whether they have stayed pure and, if so, why they are glad they did. The boldness these people shared in their responses is remarkable, and they can give us some insights into what experiencing a life of purity looks like. Check these out:

> Yes, I have stayed pure. I feel that God's plan is so much better than I can even imagine, so I'd rather wait on Him. I am so glad I've waited.
>
> **(Female, age 17)**

> I haven't had a boyfriend for a year, which really helps. I'm glad that even in past relationships I've controlled myself, because now I can give myself to my husband completely.
>
> **(Female, age 18)**

Yes, I have stayed pure. I want to save myself for my wedding night.
(Female, age 17)

Yes, and I am glad.
(Male, age 17)

I made a promise to God and myself that I would wait for my future husband. I don't want to break that promise, because I know I'll regret it.
(Female, age 16)

I haven't had sex, but I have messed around, and I don't feel pure anymore.
(Female, age 16)

I want my first time to be with my husband.
(Female, age 19)

I have stayed sexually pure, because that is the thing to do. God has really helped.
(Male, age 19)

I know sex is more than physical and that you become one with that person, so the only person I want to share that with is my husband. It's saved me from carrying a lot of hurt and baggage.
(Female, age 19)

> *Yes, I've stayed pure. I wear a purity ring, and I love my choice because it sets an example. I don't think I'm better than anyone else, but it helps me in being a leader to others. Being a Christian means worshiping God in all you do. He said sex is for marriage—and that is final!*
>
> **(Male, age 20)**

God really does have our best interests at heart when He tells us to remain pure. It's like a parent telling his or her two-year-old not to touch a hot stove. The child wants to do it anyway, but the parent knows what is best, which is why he or she tells the child not to touch the stove. You can see from the stories in the previous chapter just how many people have been burned. If you want to avoid this, just follow God's ways.

> *I have not lost my virginity because I believe it is a gift, and you can't get it back. It is very important to keep it.*
>
> **(Female, 16)**

> *I want to wait and see the woman God has picked out for me.*
>
> **(Male, age 16)**

It's very important to me to stay pure until I'm married. I know it will be worth it and that God will bless me for it.

(Female, age 15)

Sex really is a gift that God has given you to give to your spouse—and only to your spouse. It is a precious and personal part of you that only one person should ever have the privilege of seeing or experiencing. Believe me, those who wait to have sex until they get married (and I've talked to tons of them) experience the most incredible heavenly bliss of sexual pleasure. It makes a big difference when you make the choice not to listen to the world but to hold out for your future spouse.

Yes, I have stayed pure, because I made a promise to do so.

(Male, age 16)

I want to stay a virgin for my future husband. I believe that I am worth more than to give away my special gift to just anyone.

(Female, age 16)

The paradox is that while many young people give themselves away because they don't feel loved or important, the act of giving themselves away sexually actually makes them feel less and less valuable. This is why it is important to place a value on your innocence and purity. The only one who should have the privilege of knowing you in a sexual way is the one who has committed himself or herself to you for the rest of your life.

> Sadly, I have lost my virginity, but I wish I hadn't. I wish I would have stayed sexually pure so that I could give something that is precious to my husband. I don't have sex anymore, because even though I'm physically not a virgin, I am saving my body for my husband.
>
> **(Female, age 19)**

Many people have chosen to become what has been called "recycled virgins." Once they discover the truth about how God wants them to save their bodies for their future spouse, they make a commitment to live a pure and holy life from that moment on. One day, these individuals will be able to look their husband or wife right in the eye and say, "Listen, I messed up before I knew the truth, but ever since then I have been pure and kept my purity only for you." There is no shame in that.

I stayed pure because I knew that sex before
marriage would only result in pain, emptiness
and a broken heart. I knew that God asks us to stay
pure for a reason. His way is always best! I'm so
glad I did, because I see friends who had sex who
are now lonely and addicted. I am glad I
saved myself from that pain.

(Female, age 19)

I've remained a virgin because I want to live by
God's Word and be pure for my husband.

(Female, age 16)

I stayed pure because I knew that it was a sin against God not
to do so and that it was not His will for us as His creation.
I am glad I did, because I now can give myself completely to
my husband with no regrets of past experiences.

(Female, age 19)

Yes, I have stayed sexually pure. I believe the main reason is my
parents. My father set standards for me from a young age. He said,
"No dating." I understand why he did this, but it was hard. I came to
the point where I really wanted to date, but my dad came into my
room and said that he wanted me to wait as much as possible for as
long as possible. This really shaped the way I saw purity. My parents
helped me uphold a standard.

(Female, age 19)

I have stayed sexually pure as it relates to guys.
It is so great knowing that I'm not emotionally
attached or physically attached to any man. And the man
I marry will be the first guy I'll ever kiss on the lips!
Looking back on my high school relationships makes
them seem so ridiculous now!

(Female, age 19)

It's amazing how many young people are beginning to make this type of commitment. Not only are they choosing not to have sex, but they also want to have "virgin lips" when they get married because they realize the value of romance and the value of intimacy. They understand that it starts with a kiss. This idea seems pretty radical, but I know couples who have done this and have amazing marriages.

I stayed pure because I wanted to honor God
with everything—my mind, soul and body. I wanted
to save myself for my husband. I'm glad I
did, because now I have that gift to give him.

(Female, age 19)

I grew up in a Christian family, and my parents taught us that sex
was for marriage. I am glad they did, because when I get married
it will be a blessing and not a problem.

(Female, age 18)

> I stayed pure because I was always
> scared that if I didn't I was going to get sick.
> I didn't know anything.
>
> **(Male, age 20)**

> There were not very many girls where
> I come from, and I was never good friends
> with any of them. The issue never came up.
> I am very happy for that.
>
> **(Male, age 19)**

> Guys didn't like me. It wasn't hard.
>
> **(Female, age 19)**

Some have said that being beautiful as a young person can actually be a curse, because people are constantly attracted to you for the wrong reasons (for your face or body). One young lady told me that she wanted to be ugly while she was young so she could stay pure and then get prettier when she got older. Regardless of whether people find you attractive or not, you are valuable and your purity is valuable. Hold on to it.

> I believe that sex is special and should be saved for
> marriage because God's Word commands it. I am
> very glad I have made this decision. Not only does it
> save me a lot of heartache, but I'm also honoring God.
>
> **(Female, age 19)**

God knew what He was doing when He made sex
for marriage only. Relationships are broken by sex outside of
marriage. I've seen it happen. I want to stay pure for my
wife for that reason.

(Male, age 21)

I am waiting for my wife. It's going to
be the most precious moment we have.

(Male, age 20)

I have remained a virgin because I was scared. I am glad,
because now I can give my virginity to my wife.

(Male, age 20)

When I was in sixth grade I decided to
not date, because I thought dating was silly.
For this reason, I've remained sexually pure.
I'm glad I made this decision, because I
know that it praises God!

(Male, age 19)

I stayed sexually pure because I had an
indescribable deep conviction to do so.
I didn't understand why I did so at the
time, but now I see that God had been
protecting me. I am glad to be able to someday
give my future husband my purity.

(Female, age 18)

I made a decision to live a pure life
to obey the Lord and bless my future
husband. My parents, friends, fellow
churchgoers, mentors and others have
helped by watching out for me.

(Female, age 19)

I have remained sexually pure. I grew up
being taught that sex was for marriage only and
that anything other than that would only hurt me.
I, myself, was born out of wedlock, so my parents
relayed to me the heartache they went through
because of their decision. Even though by the
grace of God they are still together (they were
only 16 and 17 when they had me), I never wanted
to go through that same thing.

(Female, age 19)

A lot of people will point a finger in your face and say that
sex outside of marriage "is wrong, is wrong, is wrong," but the
truth is that "it hurts, it hurts, it hurts." Sex before marriage destroys relationships, is painful to the people involved, and can
create a potentially destructive environment for the children
who are brought into the world as a result of it.

I have chosen to remain pure because
I saw how some of my closest friends
fell apart after having sex with their
boyfriend. They thought they'd be
together forever, but a few days later
the guy would walk away.

(Female, age 19)

I was always taught that sex was for
marriage. Later, I realized that it was
something I wanted to give my wife.

(Male, age 19)

I am still a virgin, if that is the definition of
sexual purity. I was raised with the understanding
that God desires us to stay sexually pure, so I
wanted to try to please God.

(Male, age 19)

Remaining sexually pure is something asked
of me by God. I want to have that
special bond with my future husband. I am
glad I have remained pure, because I
have seen the pain caused when people
have sex before marriage.

(Female, age 20)

I've remained pure because I know that sex is more than a physical action; it also takes an emotional part of you. It is what God calls us to do.

(Female, age 19)

I didn't have sex because I was told not to—and I followed this even when I really wanted to give in. Eventually purity became a passion of mine, because "the pure in heart will see God."

(Female, age 18)

I stayed pure mostly because I was aware at a very young age of how sacred sex is and because I always knew that it was intended for marriage only. I am glad that my parents set boundaries for me when I was too young to make such decisions on my own. Through reading many books and being influenced by other Christians, I began to make choices for myself to keep myself pure. Although there were times when I was ready to date in high school—abstaining from it is one of the best things I could have done for myself—I don't regret it at all.

(Female, age 19)

Many people say that they want a relationship that is pure—one that has no dark places or secrets. The way to stay pure in a relationship is by inviting others to hold you accountable to do what you say you want to do. Many people actually come up with a document of accountability at the beginning of a boyfriend/girlfriend relationship. It's a certificate similar to the one in the back of the book in which you ask each other questions such as, "What are our standards?" "How will we treat each other?" "What is the purpose of this relationship?" Essentially, you discuss these issues and then sign the document, saying, "This is what we're all about." After this, you have your parents, your closest friends and maybe even several leaders in your life also sign the document. In this way, you are publicly saying, "We are going to date each other, but we are not sliding off the mountain into sexual immorality. We want you—the people in our lives closest to us—to hold us to our word." Once you sign it, keep it public, and ask those who signed it to keep you accountable. By being honest and open about the relationship, you will honor God through the way you're honoring each other.

What God, the Inventor of Sex, Says About Sex

Have it!

Have lots of it!

Have lots of it with the person you marry!

Sex is a good thing because God made it, and everything He made, He made good. When you follow the guidelines for sex that God intended, it is better than anything you could imagine.

Think about this a sec. How cool must God be? He could have invented anything He wanted to get more people on this earth—have them hang on trees, have them come up out of the ground, literally have storks carry them and drop them off. But when He thought of how to get more of us on the planet, He dreamed up sex. Now, if you love God for no other reason, then you should love Him for this: *God invented sex.*

Imagine you were there the day God created sex. God the Father, Son and the Holy Spirit are having a committee meeting; they are talking about the world and making humans. All of a sudden, one of them says to the others, "How are we going to get more of them?" Another of them, with a sparkle in the eye, looks across the room and says, "Are you thinking what I am thinking?" They soon start high-fiving each other, because they are so excited. "Those humans are going to have so much fun on that planet!"

So, if God is the one who thought up sex, He is the one who ought to know how to have the best sex. Let's look at a couple of guidelines He put in Scripture for us. First of all, besides making babies, what is the purpose of sex? Look at it this way: each person, way deep down inside, has something that I will call a *passion button*. You can tell when someone has his or her passion button pushed. You see it when you are flipping through the channels on your TV. You see when you are watching a movie in the theater. Someone will be making out with someone else; he or she will be sweating and passionately involved in the scene. You can tell that someone has pushed his or her passion button.

Different things push different people's passion buttons. Holding hands, a lingering kiss or an arm around someone can trigger it. For guys, it might be something they look at. We have all seen the classic scenario of an old man ogling a young lady until he gets whiplash in his neck. Just looking at her activates his passion button.

So, what is the purpose of this passion button? Inscribe this on your heart: *God gave you a passion button so that you would have a passionate way of expressing your love to the person you are committed to for the rest of your life.* God gave you that button with the intent that only one person should ever get to push it, and no one else should ever have the privilege of seeing it pushed. Not a girlfriend, not a boyfriend. Not somebody you are dating, not a one-night stand, not a long-term relationship, not even somebody to whom you are engaged. Not a magazine, not a movie, not a TV program or something you see on the Internet. Only the person you are married to.

God wanted you to be able to passionately express your love to that person in a way like no one else in your life. The problem is that if you don't know the purpose of the passion button that God has given you, you won't use it for the right reason. Like many people, you may have had your passion button pushed so many different times for so many different reasons that you don't even realize why God gave it to you. But now you do.

Take it from someone who has been married for 25 years: When you follow God's commands, sex never gets boring, and it never gets dry. God *wants* you to have the greatest sex possible, which is why the Bible talks about living in *absolute purity*—keeping yourself for the person you will one day marry. Song of Solomon 8:4 states, "Do not arouse or awaken love until it so desires." In other words, don't awaken the passion side of love until it's the right time. Regardless of how the world (or a boyfriend, or a girlfriend, or the peer pressure from your friends) tries to push your passion button, don't awaken that passion until the right time: your wedding night. That part of you should just stay asleep and not be woken up until the proper time when you are committed to another person in marriage.

Any other involvement in sex has the potential to destroy what God designed to be amazing. Whether it is looking at pornography, touching another's private places or whatever else, all of that is reserved for only the person you will marry. This is why it is so important to commit your eyes to purity. Even as Job said, "I make a covenant with my eyes not to look lustfully at a girl," make a covenant with your eyes, saying, "I am not going to look at it or have anything to do with it."

Please see the purity certificate at the end of this book, where you will have a chance to make this commitment. Remember that when you make this pledge, you are not just making it to God but you are also making it to the person whom you are going to marry. You probably don't even know who that person will be right now. In effect, you are saying, "I am going to keep my body for you. I am going to starve my passion button for you. I am not going to let anybody or anything push my passion button except you on the night of our wedding."

This is how God invented sex to be used, and boy, when it is done right, there is nothing the world has to offer that comes close to God's original.

What Those Who Waited Say About Sex

As previously mentioned, most of the sex that we see on TV and in the movies is between single people. In fact, in one analysis of the major networks shows at the start of the 2007-2008 season, references to unmarried sex outnumbered references to married sex by a 2 to 1 margin.[1] In another analysis conducted by a conservative special-interest group, during one primetime period in the fall of 2007, verbal references to non-marital sex outnumbered references to sex in marriage by nearly a 3 to 1 margin. Scenes implying sex between unmarried partners outnumbered similar scenes between married couples 4 to 1.[2]

With the amount of sex we see between single people on TV and in the movies, you would think that sleeping around with all kinds of different people would be the most exciting lifestyle possible. Whether it's a teen movie or *Sex and the City* or *Friends*, sex is portrayed as the ultimate rush. These people all act like they are having the greatest time, and they never seem to suffer any consequences for their actions. On the other hand, most marriages on TV are portrayed as old fashioned, uneventful and, basically, a snore. But is this an accurate picture? I think it's about time we listened to the ones who really know what they're talking about.

In fact, when you look at the real data and talk to real people about their marriage and their sex life, it's a completely different story. For instance, one study conducted by the Minnesota Family Council found that married people are way happier than unmarried people. When asked why this is the case, one of the researchers for the project stated:

> If you ask people in the survey how happy they are in general, *married people say they are happier than unmarried people.* They are less likely to be lonely or depressed, or to abuse drugs or alcohol than single people, and all these problems lead to unhappiness. And married people always have someone who cares about them to talk to.[3]

The researcher went on to say that both married men and women are mentally and emotionally happier.

One of the other myths about marriage this study exposed was that married people lead boring lives without much "action." On this point, they went on to say, "A number of recent studies that have asked people detailed questions about their sex lives show *that married men and women are much more sexually active than single men and women.*"[4] Did you get that? Married people are *more* sexually active. They are even happier than single people who have a sex partner. And studies also show that married women are almost twice as likely as divorced or unmarried women to have a sex life that is extremely emotionally satisfying.[5]

So, what culture tries to tell us—that the only way to have a great sex life is by sleeping with lots of different people—is actually the *opposite* of what produces real happiness. People who are married have way more sex, and they are way happier with the sex that they have.

Some might say, "Wait a minute, can't you be just as happy if you live together and have sex?" The Minnesota Family Council study also found that this was not true. A second researcher for the project stated:

Co-habitors [those who just live together] don't have relationships that are as warm and loving as most married people. Especially cohabiting men who are not engaged—they have less commitment to their partners than husbands. Co-habitors have more conflict and a less satisfying relationship than married couples. This is both a cause and consequence of avoiding marriage.

And the research shows they just don't get the same benefits in terms of health, longevity, wealth and mental health that married couples do.[6]

Other studies demonstrate this same point. In one study conducted by Dr. Linda J. Waite, professor of sociology at the University of Chicago, research showed that both men and women are happier with their sex lives once they are married. In fact, Dr. Waite states that "married people have sex twice as often as single people." Did you catch that? *Twice as often* as single people. She goes on to state that "unmarried couples who live together also have active sex lives but, like unmarried people, get less emotional satisfaction from it than married people."[7] In other words, while unmarried couples who live together also have active sex lives, they get *less emotional satisfaction* from sex than do married people. The study also showed that for married men, frequency of sex, fidelity and emotional commitment to the relationship led to greater satisfaction. These elements are equally important to women, but the mere fact of being married also tends to contribute to their levels of satisfaction. "Men make an investment in pleasing their partner because of the ongoing relationship," Dr. Waite states. "People who are committed to a partner get more than sex out of sex."[8]

So, not only are married people a lot happier because they are having more sex, but their emotional happiness is off the charts because of the life-long commitment they make to each other. And there are a lot of other benefits as well: People who are married tend to be financially well off, are psychologically more balanced, are less likely to have psychological dysfunction, and are less likely to abuse alcohol, marijuana and cocaine. They also tend to be much happier later in life, as opposed to those who divorce later in life thinking they would be happier if they were single.

As you can see, the data is clear. Even secular researchers have to admit that people who are married their entire lives have a lot more sex and a better sex life. The point is that God knew exactly what He was doing when He gave us instructions to save our bodies for the one with whom we will be married. He gave us these commands because He *wants* us to have a great sex life.

God's teenage guide to a healthy sex life is simple: Don't have sex. Wait until you are married, and then give all your passion and all your love to the one you are going to be committed to for the rest of your life. This is God's recipe for the most amazing sex life ever invented in the history of mankind. And the studies show that God was right after all!

What Tempted People Say About Sex

By now, I hope you are convinced that it is best to wait for marriage to have sex. Now the big question is, how can we overcome the firehose of sexual temptation that is aimed at us? How do we stay pure? There are boyfriends and girlfriends pressuring us. We've got everybody and their brother telling us how great it is to fool around. The world is painting this picture of how great sex is, and many of us are craving love and intimacy. So how in the world do we stay pure?

In this chapter, you will hear from some guys and girls who were actually in situations where they felt pressured to say yes to sex. You'll hear how they responded to the pressure and what advice they have to give to others. Check out what they have to say.

Have You Ever Been Pressured to Have Sex and Said No?

There are a lot of heroes out there—a lot of young men and women who decided to stay pure even when pressured to go down the wrong path. It's easy to stay pure when you are alone in your room by yourself. But when you are with a guy or girl in a situation that is less than optimal . . . then it's easy to become swayed. Here are some stories of victory.

Yes. My girlfriend at the time really started pressuring me to do more, but I said no. It would have been a big deal to my mom, and I didn't want to face the consequences. I also knew that it says no sex before marriage in the Bible.

(Male, age 16)

I was pressured by an ex-girlfriend who was in college. She wanted to have a kid, and I was only 15 at the time. She kept asking me constantly. After a year and a half, I ended the relationship.

(Male, age 17)

When I was in school, there was a guy who liked me, and he was always after me. He was really nice, but then he started to come on to me sexually. When I said no, he never spoke to me again.

(Female, age 20)

My girlfriend wanted to have sex, and I said no.

(Male, age 17)

One time, my boyfriend (who said he would never pressure me) told me it would be okay to have sex because we were so in love and we would do it at some point or another. When I said no, he said that I didn't really love him. He got over it, and I'm really happy we didn't have sex, because now we're not even together.

(Female, age 16)

Me and a girl were on a bed making out. My cousin and my brother were playing X-box in front of us. I said no.

(Male, age 19)

I was with some friends. Things got weird, and I was asked to have sex. I left. I mean, I was out!

(Male, age 15)

I've been pressured plenty of times. I was always the nice guy in high school, respected by the girls. So they threw it at me countless times, saying, "I trust you." I always said, "No, because I respect you!"

(Male, age 20)

I have been pressured by a guy friend. I made a bad choice of watching a movie with him alone at my house. And I said no.

(Female, age 16)

I was pressured into having sex one time, but I knew that the immediate pleasure would never amount to the life-long displeasure that was to come.

(Male, age 16)

Yes. I said no to my first love, and he and I decided not to stay together. He went and slept with my friend right away.

(Female, age 19)

Too many young people give their heart away, and then their body follows. Fortunately, this young lady was smart enough not to give away her body. The Bible talks about us guarding our hearts because out of it comes the wellspring of life (see Proverbs 3:23). So be careful about letting your heart go, because when your heart goes first it's harder to stop your body from following.

I haven't been pressured, but I've told people no.

(Female, age 16)

My ex wanted to fool around, but I didn't really want to. Guys will try to do things and manipulate you to get you in the mood.

(Female, age 22)

My friend's girlfriend wanted to have oral sex, but I said I wouldn't do that.

(Male, age 20)

When I had a girlfriend, she tried to get me to have sex, but I listened to God and resisted.

(Male, age 20)

I was at a friend's house one time and he began to tell me that he had liked me for a long time and that he loved me. I told him no, and after a long argument I called my mom and she came to get me.

(Female, age 19)

My boyfriend wanted to go "all the way," but I said no. He broke up with me. End of story.

(Female, age 19)

my aunt's boyfriend raped me about five months ago. I thought it was my fault that I led him on, and then he got me alone and took advantage of me. I said no. I tried to fight back, but I got tired and laid there numb while he took my virginity from me.

(Female, age 17)

Obviously, the precious young lady in this last story is not to blame for what happened. This perverted older guy just could not control himself. She tried to fight back; she tried to say no. If this has happened to you, you need to understand that as far as God is concerned, you are still pure. The best path of freedom is to forgive the person and ask God to wash your memory. I know of girls who were brutally raped. Once they chose to forgive the guy responsible, they were able to recount the whole incident without a tear. They have the memory, but they don't have the pain because God healed their heart and the memory.

Advice from Those Who Kept Their Purity

We asked these guys and girls who are living in the battlefield but have managed to avoid the temptation to have sex to give some advice on how to keep your purity. Here is what they said.

Draw the boundary at just a kiss. People say that making out is okay, but it only leads to the next thing. It does not matter how great of a Christian you are. When things get heated, you are less likely to stop. Even saving kissing until marriage would help.

(Female, age 18)

My parents always told me to save myself until marriage. It was as if the world was gonna end if I didn't, so it kinda scared me.

(Female, age 17)

Don't put yourself in tempting situations, and do not advertise yourself.

(Female, age 17)

Never be alone for long periods of time! Stay out of relationships. Have a line drawn that you never go past.

(Female, age 18)

Just know that if a guy is trying to have sex with you before you are married, he doesn't respect you—and he never will.

(Female, age 17)

Find some people who share and value their virginity and stick to them. Really talk to them when you are being tempted.

(Female, age 20)

Just stay close to God and His Word.

(Male, age 19)

Just remember that even though you think your guy is different, he's not. Guys will tell you whatever you want to hear to get what they want.

(Female, age 19)

Don't chill along with the opposite sex. Keep accountable with a same-gender friend.

(Male, age 20)

Don't follow the trend, and listen to people who are well educated in God and His Word.

(Male, age 16)

Don't go places with a guy or girl alone! Group dates are a lot of fun.

(Female, age 16)

Do not tempt yourself by kissing or doing anything more than holding hands. Sometimes even holding hands can lead you into sin.

(Female, age 19)

Avoid alone time in a house, car or bedroom.

(Female, age 17)

Remember that your virginity is a special gift-the best gift you can give your future spouse.

(Female, age 16)

Girls, close your legs.
Boys, keep it in your pants.

(Male, age 17)

Don't get into a relationship unless you're ready to get married. Wear modest clothing, not clothes that will draw guys' attention to your body parts (like having your cleavage showing).

(Female, age 19)

Warn the person before you date him or her that you plan on no sex.

(Female, age 16)

Don't do anything you wouldn't do around your parents. Set standards early in the relationship of what is not okay. Don't sit in the car alone. Do things with other people. Ask someone to keep you accountable.

(Female, age 19)

PARENTS! They must be involved.
They need to ask their kids questions and know what's really going on. All teens have questions about what is okay sexually, but who answers their questions is probably the deciding factor.

(Female, age 19)

Let God be your true and ultimate satisfaction. Abide in His Word, and let it consume your life with truth!

(Female, age 19)

If you catch yourself looking at the wrong thing, just bounce your eyes to a still object in the room. For example, if you're dining, look at the saltshaker real quick.

(Male, age 19)

"Bouncing your eyes" is a trend that is becoming popular among men who want to stay pure. When you see something that tempts you, look up. Look at the floor. If you are walking past Victoria's Secret in the mall, or if you're at the beach, just bounce your eyes. You and your friends can even keep each other accountable in this. Maybe you are walking past something and someone says, "Okay, guys, bounce your eyes." You can't help the first glance, but you sure can help the second one. This will help you not grow into a perverted guy, and it also protects your heart.

Have an accountability system with your closest friends. Help each other.

(Female, age 19)

Just understand that it is not for you; it was made for a different season of your life, not this one.

(Female, age 18)

Don't kiss before marriage! Don't do anything that will push your passion "button." Don't date, and stay away from porn and teenage girl mags.

(Female, age 22)

Have your standards set—know your convictions and make them line up with God's Word.

(Female, age 18)

I have never even dated, which generally
helps a lot. Find a godly older person who can
council you and find a friend (of the same
gender) who can hold you accountable. Trust the
Lord and know that He is good and will one
day give you the gift with your spouse—
and that it will not hurt.

(Female, age 19)

When in a relationship, don't do anything that
makes you want to go further physically, even if it
means you don't even hold hands.

(Female, age 19)

Guard your mind/thoughts. Even things like
watching impure movies or TV can get your mind
going places you would never want to go.

(Female, age 20)

Second Timothy 2:22 says to FLEE all youthful lusts. "Flee"
means get out of town as if your life depended on it. In fact, why
don't you just scream it out right now as loud as you can:
"FLEEEEEEEEEEEEEEEEEE!" I can't tell you how many guys
and girls I have talked to who wish right before they blew it one
of them had screamed "NO" as loud as they could.

The smarter thing is to make sure you don't get into that situation. Don't get in the car alone with a guy or girl; have some other friends around you. Don't be at your girlfriend's or boyfriend's house or in a room alone. Look at how many tragic stories there are of people who got caught up in the moment and gave away their purity. They happened to be at the wrong place at the wrong time, and their parents weren't there. Maybe they were at a party or alone in a back bedroom. It all starts with a set-up.

So be smart about where you go and what you do. Have conviction in your heart about saving your purity for the one you will spend the rest of your life with in marriage! That is the key to a lifelong great sex life!

13

What Curious People Say About Sex

In this chapter, I have accumulated a number of common questions from young people about sex. I will do my best to answer them.

My mom basically said that she would buy me birth control if I could handle myself. So why not do it?
(Female, age 19)

Just because your parents allow you to do something does not mean that it's the right thing to do. They may be struggling with guilt from the past. They may not understand the purpose of the passion button and how great a sex life you can have if you stay pure and get married to your lifelong partner. Hopefully, you have seen through some of the stories in this book why not to do it. Look at all the heartbreak and catastrophe you avoid by not having sex and all the pleasure and ecstasy you experience by saving yourself for your future husband or wife.

How does sex correlate to our spiritual
relationship with the Lord?

(Female, age 19)

In 1 Corinthians 6:18-19, Paul says that the person who commits sexual immorality sins against his or her own body. He also talks about how the body is the temple of the Holy Spirit. We only hurt ourselves when we emotionally bond to someone else outside of marriage. God hates sin because it not only breaks His heart but also destroys our lives. He does not want us to be destroyed. Committing sexual sin means breaking the moral code that God put inside us, which separates us from God and destroys our lives.

Will there be sex in heaven?
If so, with who?

(Female, age 19)

Jesus said that there will not be any marriage in heaven (see Matthew 22:30). The Bible doesn't say exactly if there will be sex in heaven, but I do know that heaven will be *better* than sex. God is so awesome and amazing, and we will be thrilled with whatever is there. He has been preparing it for us a long time, and it will blow our minds!

Why did the world turn sex into a
nasty thing to do?
(Female, age 19)

When people don't know the purpose for something, they use it the wrong way. If you did not know the purpose of a guitar and someone talked to you about playing baseball, you might be tempted to use the guitar as a baseball bat and destroy it. That is exactly what has happened with sex. People don't know the purpose of it, so they use it in all the wrong ways. As a result, we have this perversity in our society that seems to increase as the days go by. It's a bunch of blind people leading the blind, and none of them ever come close to the truth. Sex is a beautiful thing when done God's way in the context of marriage. Everything God made is good.

How do I keep my mind pure and not just
my body? How do I know how far is too far?
(Female, age 19)

Keeping your mind pure is a matter of making decisions to set your mind on things above. With all the sexual messages bombarding you through the Internet, cell phones, radios and everything else, you have to choose to look at the right things, watch the right things, and not watch the wrong things. How can those in the world tell you about sex when they did not invent it? Every time you watch something that has a lovemaking scene in it, it's giving you an idea of what Hollywood or the porn industry thinks love is all about. You need to be smarter than that. Look away. Walk away. Shut it off. Fast-forward. Do something so you are not standing at the edge of the cliff hoping you do not fall off. The goal is not to just avoid falling off the cliff but to actually walk away from the edge of the cliff.

Think about it like this: Your whole body is reserved as an amazing treasure for the person you will marry. All of your personal parts, including emotions and private parts, are supposed to be reserved for the one with whom you spend the rest of your life. Anyone who touches your private parts interferes with your future husband's or wife's privilege—a privilege that only he or she should have. Sex is precious, beautiful and amazing, but you can only experience it to its fullest if you make sure you only give it as a gift to the one you will marry.

Does sex hurt?
(Female, age 16)

This is a common question in the back of people's mind (particularly girls). When you are engaged to be married, there are materials you can read and premarital counselors you can talk to who can help you make sure that your first sexual experience is blissful, peaceful, enjoyable and pretty much without pain. Those details are not necessary for you to know right now. If YOU wait and get godly advice from your mother, father and a premarital counselor, they will give you advice to make sure that your first time will be amazing.

> Why is having sex such a bad thing? How does it affect me if I don't get pregnant or an STD?
> **(Female, age 16)**

Even if you don't get pregnant or contract an STD, there will always be emotional consequences. You think having sex will make you feel loved, but it will only end up making you feel used. If you have had sex outside marriage, you need to get whole again and healed in your heart. God can do that if you turn it over to Him. Remember that sex is not a bad thing when it's done God's way, but it will destroy you if it is not used the way God designed for it to be used.

> Why do you have to have an emotional connection with everyone you sleep with? Can't you just do it with no strings attached?
> **(Female, age 16)**

Doing it with "no strings attached" is basically what dogs, cats, cows and other animals do. We, as humans, are not in the animal class but in the God class. We are made differently. As we mentioned earlier, we have a moral code that has been placed inside of us. God meant sex for humans to be way better than anything any animal could experience. Like it or not, whenever there is sexual involvement an emotional connection is made, even if it is between "friends with benefits." The sacredness is stolen. That sacredness can only be restored by asking forgiveness from God and committing to reserve yourself for the person you marry.

Is it okay with God if you
kiss before marriage?

(Female, age 15)

In 1 Corinthians 10:23, Paul said all things are possible, but not all things are wise. In fact, there are many couples who decide not to kiss until they are married. The reason is because there is an implied covenant when you kiss. It takes a little bit of your purity and a little of your innocence. It's a level of affection given away that maybe should be reserved. In addition, all too often people start kissing, and then it leads to other things. Regardless, I don't think God necessarily has an opinion. It might be wise for you to consider your own "passion button" (see chapter 9). If kissing pushes your passion button, then don't do it. Don't go near the edge of the cliff and then try not to fall off. Stay as far away from it as you can.

How do you get free from sexual addictions?
(Female, age 18)

You have to start new habits. You have to get some accountability. You have to stop looking at things you have been looking at. You have to get protection for your computer by putting on some Internet filters such as Net Nanny®, Safe Eyes®, CYBERsitter® or PureSight®. Then you need to go deeper and figure out what your real need is. What is driving you to keep going back to the addiction? Are you using sex as a way to numb some hidden pain? If so, you may want to get help from a counselor or support group or pick up some resources that can help you work through the real issues without resorting to addictive behaviors.

If you are involved in a relationship where you feel you have to have sex all the time, the love and intimacy and emotional quotient you are longing for is not found there. Go to Jesus. He will meet all your needs.

Why is sex so addicting? Why is it
such a struggle to overcome pornography
or sleeping around?
(Gender and age unknown)

Whether it's looking at pornography or having sex, each of us has an inner drive that motivates us to want sex. We like the feeling we get at the moment. The problem is, as you can see from all these stories, no matter how great the feeling is at the time, if we don't do it in the context of marriage, we end up with a *massive* sense of emptiness. It's almost like doing cocaine or another drug. We like it for the moment, but between hits we are miserable. We keep thinking that one more high will make up for all the misery we feel, but it certainly does not.

What Sexually Confused People Say About Sex

You have probably heard the Katy Perry song, "I Kissed a Girl." One of the verses talks about how she doesn't even know the girl's name she is kissing, but that it doesn't matter because the girl is just an "experimental game." After all, it's just "human nature."

This is just one of many messages people receive through music and television that confuses their sexual identity. We now have people growing up who are wondering, *Was I born gay or straight?* We have people like Katy Perry telling us that kissing someone of the same sex doesn't really mean you're gay—you're just experimenting and playing around. This only leads to more and more confusion and brokenness.

For the past 30 to 40 years, there has been a push from the gay community to make the idea that someone could be born gay a common thought. They have been pushing to make the gay lifestyle more and more acceptable. Just look at the number of references to the gay lifestyle in popular TV programs, movies and songs during the last 30 to 40 years. They have become way more common and more acceptable.

Are People Born Gay?

This is a critical question. Some gay activists have theorized that there *might* be a "gay gene"—and almost everyone just took this to be absolute truth; but in fact no such gene has ever been discovered. In fact, there have been many studies done that have said there is *no possible way* a person could be born gay. Even homosexuals who have done research themselves have not been able to come up with a definitive conclusion as to whether people are born gay or straight. In one study conducted by gay scientists, researchers looked at identical twins. They reasoned that if there is a gay gene, then if one twin thought he or she was gay, the other would as well. What they found is that there are many identical twins in which one twin insists he or she is gay while the other is not. So it is impossible to say that a person's genes will cause him or her to be gay. As a result of much of this research, in 2008 the American Psychological Association put out a revised publication that included an admission that there is no gay gene.

Yet the fact remains that many people feel attracted to the same sex. One 18-year-old girl said the following:

Just last year I fell into a situation I would never have imagined. My best friend (a female) and I started becoming very physical in our relationship, and it definitely became inappropriate and sinful quickly. God told me to cut off my friendship, and emotionally it has been the hardest thing I've ever had to deal with. I definitely regret the sinful choices I made. They have caused much hurt and pain for me, my friend, my family and many others. But God has certainly used this past year for so much good and healing and restoration for both of us. But it's been hard—there was definitely a soul-tie to be broken!

Why Do Some People Believe They Are Gay?

Some people, even from the time they were young, have genuinely felt that they were born gay. They have felt this way their entire lives. So, why would they feel that way if they were not truly born that way? There are a couple of possible reasons.

- *Abuse.* Some people may have been abused when they were younger. The abuser could have been a person of the same or opposite sex. If a little boy is abused by an older perverted man, it can play games with his mind. As he grows up, he begins to think, *What is it about me that attracted that man to me? Something is wrong with me . . . maybe I'm gay.* When a little girl is molested by an older man, it often results in a deep hatred for men, and she begins to believe that men will always take advantage of her. She often has *no* emotional attachment from her father or any other male. She ends up feeling that the only way she can get love and satisfaction is from a female.

· *Emotional detachment (males).* One reason why boys might begin to feel they are gay is because of a relationship gap between son and father. For various reasons, the father does not know how to be close to his son. In such cases, many times the son will latch on to his mother emotionally, identify with her, and start to display some effeminate qualities. Maybe the father does not know how to be affectionate, has never said I love you, or has never given his son a hug. Sometimes when guys do not get that from their dad, they begin to look for unhealthy affection from other males. As a result, they feel attracted to other guys in an unhealthy way in order to get affection from them. The truth is that we were all designed with a need for a healthy relationship with our mom and dad. I have a 14-year-old son whom I have kissed on the head his whole life and told him how much I love him and appreciate him. As males, we need affection from our dads, and it needs to be healthy, wholesome fatherly affection.

- *Emotional detachment (females).* The same thing can happen to little girls who have never really bonded with their dad and never had wholesome affection from their father. It affects them one of two ways: (1) They might go out looking for unhealthy affection from guys, giving their body and heart away to whatever guy will show them affection; and (2) they might shield themselves from all guys, because they don't want to get hurt and don't feel like they can be close to any guy. In such cases, they might look for emotional closeness with a female.

- *Living in a fallen world.* We live in a fallen world with lots of temptations luring us in every direction, and there may not be a clear explanation as to why some people fall into this sin any more than why some people rob banks or lie to others. We don't have to explain the *why* for every sin and every issue in life; we just can be assured of Jesus' love and forgiveness when we turn away from any sin issue in our lives!

The fact is that just because the culture says it is okay to experiment and you might have played around, it doesn't mean that you are gay. This is not to say that it is a wise thing to do or that it will be helpful in any way. We need to avoid confusion as much as we can—especially sexual confusion—but it's important to recognize that one doesn't lead to the other.

Our Response

We live in an age where Satan lies to people about who they are, and our culture has made it socially acceptable to live a gay lifestyle freely and openly. Everyone struggles with sin, and many people live sinful lifestyles, but not one of us has the right to judge another person. For those of us who say we follow Christ, it is very important that we don't judge other people because of their sexual preference. They are just confused, and they are hurting, and we have been called to love them and show them who Jesus is.

In fact, our hearts should go out to them, because, as we have seen, many of these individuals have been victimized in some way and are leading emotionally battered lives. Instead of being mean to them or using vile words against them, we need to seek to understand them and get to know them. The reality is that these individuals are a lot more than just their sexual identity. If they think they are gay, that is just one part of them. They are spiritual, they are intellectual, and they have gifts and talents.

Jesus came to save, to serve and to give life. It's interesting to note that in the places where He speaks harshly to people in the Bible, He's actually talking to those who identify themselves as "God's people" but aren't really loving others (see Matt. 15:1-3,12-13; 16:6; 23:1-36; John 2:13-16). He doesn't call out the ones who aren't yet His own. In the same way, we should obey God and show people the way to Jesus. Jesus will change them, make them whole, and transform them into who they should be. NOT US.

So if you know someone who is struggling with this issue, get to know that person as an individual instead of pointing the judgmental finger at him or her. Seek to get to know his or her *heart*, because that is the part that Jesus really wants to change. Once He changes our hearts, He can then go to work on the rest of our lifestyle and attitudes.

What Porn Users Say About Sex

It is obvious that there is an epidemic of pornography in our culture and around the world. Pornography is addicting. It binds people like chains and destroys their marriages before they even start. As we mentioned in the last chapter, it's like a drug—an "erotic toxin"—that makes people feel high, which is why it becomes so physically addicting.

We've got to be smarter than the people who put the pornography out there and recognize that pornography can put us into bondage. We need to protect our future marriage and our future spouses from the thoughts that want to destroy our sex life before we even get married.

In this chapter, we will look at some young people who started some bad habits involving pornography and get a little advice from them on what they did to get out of it. Listen to what they have to say.

My brother introduced me to Internet porn
when I was in elementary school, and after that
I was hooked. I wanted to find out more about
the opposite sex, and I began to search out avenues.

(Male, age 19)

I was into porn for a while until
God saved me from it. I got into it
by seeing an ad on TV.

(Male, age 15)

My addiction started with
masturbation. When I was about 13,
I had to run to God so He could purify
me and take that desire away.

(Female, age 19)

When I was in middle school, I was
involved in masturbation and pornography.
This stemmed from reading romance
novels. I quickly realized that
what I was doing was wrong, and I
had repented by high school.

(Female, age 19)

When I was in junior high and a little of high school, I would get online and talk to random guys who wanted to have "cyber sex" with me. I would do this fairly regularly.

(Female, age 18)

I started using porn at a very young age when my friend showed it to me. I have gotten over it by renewing my mind daily with the Word of God and relying on Him and His faithfulness, not on my own strength.

(Male, age 19)

Porn . . . cybersex (Internet chat) . . . television, over the phone . . . "experimenting" with the same sex. I'm getting over it by the grace of God.

(Female, age 19)

It started with masturbation. My high school health teacher encouraged us to "get to know our bodies." I overcame it by memorizing a lot of Scripture— knowing who I am and what I'm worth.

(Female, age 18)

I would watch movies with inappropriate content. I was in love with the idea of being in love. Even if I was thinking about doing those things with my future husband, that still doesn't cut it. "It's still in your mind, and the journey from your mind to your hand is shorter than you're thinking" (Casting Crown's).

(Female, age 15)

My porn addiction started from emails and quickly escalated. Praying and reading my Bible has helped me-keeping my spirit man strong.

(Male, age 19)

I used to struggle with porn, but now I don't watch TV or get on the Internet unless someone is home.

(Female, age 15)

I was curious about porn when I was 11 to 12, but I never had the guts to watch it. I did struggle with masturbation. As I got older and grew in my relationship with God, the bad habits and thoughts gradually faded.

(Female, age 19)

I was into online porn. I took
my computer out of my room and have
an accountability friend.

(Male, age 20)

I never got into porn, but I remember
the first time I heard dirty jokes.
It was actually on a mission trip. They all
ended in some sexual punch line. I didn't
really know they were "dirty jokes," and I
thought it was funny to tell them.

(Female, age 19)

I was into "light" Christian romance novels
(they were definitely sexually arousing, or at
least made me sexually aware) and chick
flicks that made me constantly think about
relationships and sensuality. I'm over it now.

(Female, age 19)

It was into Internet porn and videos when
my friends would have it around. It started in
the sixth grade, cruisin' the Internet, and in
ninth grade my friends would watch it.

(Female, age 22)

For me, it was Internet pornography and being flirtatious.
It started when I accidentally walked in on my older
brother looking at some porn. I got curious, so I got
into it as well. I got over it and am still learning by setting
my mind on things above (see Colossians 3:1–2) and being
transformed by the renewing of my mind (see Romans 12:2).
I've trusted God to get me through.

(Male, age 19)

I have always struggled with lust. I have not
totally gotten over it yet.

(Male, age 19)

I used to look at porn online a lot and try to
find it on TV late at night. One day I realized
that God was better than that. I still get tempted,
but my faith drowns out the temptations.

(Male, age 22)

For me, it was Internet porn.
I don't remember how it got started.
I got to a point I hated it, so I
did whatever it took to break free
from the addiction. I read books,
told my parents, and prayed.

(Male, age 20)

When I was in middle school, I was involved in masturbation and pornography. This stemmed from romance novels. I quickly realized this was wrong and had repented by high school.

(Female, age 19)

I started masturbating when I was little. I prayed to God and asked to not have that feeling anymore, and I kept my mind pure.

(Female, age 19)

My struggle with Internet porn started out of curiosity. I wanted to know what it was all about, and I couldn't stop doing it. I got over it by seeking help for my addiction and memorizing Scripture.

(Male, age 19)

I struggled with masturbation after reading about some things and hearing that all the popular girls did it at school. I prayed that the Lord would purify my heart and sanctify my mind. We renew our minds by the Word.

(Female, age 18)

I was into pornography. It started when I slept over at a friend's house and his parents weren't home. He wanted to show me something, and it was porn. It was awkward in the beginning, but it soon became common to me. I have gotten over it by soaking in the Word. I realized that it wasn't worth it and that only God can fill my desires.

(Male, age 18)

As you can see, using pornography is destructive, and sometimes it doesn't take much to get hooked to it. It's better to stop before you ever get involved. Set up some safeguards on your computer and your phone to block certain content, and get some accountability. Put Scriptures around your computer of who you want to be. Here are a few you can use:

> *Above all else, guard your heart,*
> *for it is the wellspring of life.*
>
> **(Proverbs 4:23)**

> *Flee from sexual immorality. All other sins a man*
> *commits are outside his body, but he who sins*
> *sexually sins against his own body.*
>
> **(1 Corinthians 6:18)**

Set your minds on things above,
not on earthly things.

(Colossians 3:2)

It is God's will that you should be sanctified:
that you should avoid sexual immorality.

(1 Thessalonians 4:3)

Flee the evil desires of youth, and pursue
righteousness, faith, love and peace, along with those
who call on the Lord out of a pure heart.

(2 Timothy 2:22)

Write these verses on sticky notes and put them around your desktop so that you can remind yourself of the pure man or woman that you really want to be.

What Your Older Peeps Say About Sex

The fact is that God invented sex, and He has a lot to say about it. The Bible tells us in John 8:32 that if we hold to His teachings, we will know the truth, and the truth will set us free. The truth *always* sets us free, but if we don't know the truth, it cannot set us free. Hopefully, you have learned some truths from the stories you have heard in this book. In this final chapter, you will hear from those in your own generation about how to stay pure and set apart for God. They will speak to you as if they were sitting down and speaking with you face to face, or as if you had an older brother or sister looking you right in the eye giving you advice. Listen to what they have to say.

First and foremost, pursue the heart and will of God! Apart from Him there is no good. Build relationship with Him and seek His heart—find out His plan for romance, sexuality and purity. There is so much freedom and

protection in purity! We need strong men to rise
up and change the current of our media and culture; men
who will value and protect women and promote them rather
than perversion; fathers who will love and protect their
daughters; gentlemen who will show women their value
and treat them with respect.

(Female, age 19)

No matter how much you think you are ready for sex
or how much you're in love, you need to wait.

(Female, age 19)

Save yourself from unnecessary pain
and heartbreak. Stay emotionally and
physically pure so that you can look back
to your teenage years with no regrets.

(Male, age 19)

Don't go through what I have
gone through!

(Female, age 19)

Porn is a trap. Nothing good will come of it.

(Male, age 20)

Waiting is the best...all of my friends who had sex are not with the same guy today. It will be worth it.

(Female, age 19)

Fight to stay pure. It's worth it; you're worth it. Understand God's love for you so you won't want impurity.

(Female, age 18)

If you want to stay pure physically, you have to stay pure mentally and emotionally. If your thoughts and heart are always thinking lustfully, or if you are always reading about sex or watching it on TV, you will naturally head in that direction. Make every effort to be as pure as possible, in every way possible. There is no other way to make it.

(Female, age 18)

Stay pure. If your friends try to pressure you into having sex or tell you that it's okay to have sex before marriage, then they aren't real friends. They need to be exposed to the light. Stand up for what's right, even if you are standing alone!

(Male, age 18)

The consequences of having sex before marriage involve so much more than just possibly getting pregnant or getting an STD. It creates an emotional and physical attachment that is just overwhelming and baggage thats so hard to let go of.

(Female, age 19)

When you wait for your future husband or wife, you will have no skeletons in your past to haunt you. You can only find your fulfillment in God. He adds the rest.

(Female, age 19)

Fight for your purity! Don't put yourself in a situation that will take away your purity.

(Female, age 19)

Be the girl that God wants you to be. Remember that God has a wonderful plan for you, and you don't want to settle for second best. Wait not only on your future husband but, more importantly, on God.

(Female, age 17)

Stay strong. There will always be temptations in life that you are not going to be able to face on our own. God is always there. If He doesn't answer your prayers right away, there is a reason. If our generation doesn't fix things, then who will? Soon it will be too late.

(Female, age 16)

"Messing around" is not staying pure. If you think having sex is the only thing that will haunt you, flood your spirit with guilt and tear your life apart, you're dead wrong. Every day I have to live with the regret of "messing around." IT HURTS! But God is working on my guilt, and how I love Him! After turning my back on my former way of life, He scooped me up and is restoring me.

(Female, age 15)

I have struggled; I have cried; I have done almost everything bad you could do. But there is a God who loves me. He looks past my faults and uses my troubles to help me understand what other people are going through.

(Female, age 16)

I want my generation to be pure and seek the Lord with all their hearts. We set the standard for the next generation. If we are not following the Word of God, then why should they?

(Female, age 18)

Today's media has altered people's perceptions of sex. It would be amazing if we could view sex as something intimate with our spouse and feel no shame about it.

(Female, age 18)

My dad tells me that if you have sex or anything before marriage, you're cheating on your future spouse.

(Female, age 17)

Just wait. I have had so many friends come to me crying because they lost their virginity. Don't make the same mistake.

(Female, age 17)

If a guy is pressuring you to have sex, then he has no self-control. He can't wait until marriage, so obviously he just wants to use you.

(Female, age 16)

Don't let your guard down. Set boundaries
for yourself. Something can happen
so quickly! Hold yourself accountable.
Don't buy into the world's lies. God is the
only absolute truth.

(Female, age 17)

Wait to have sex. I've seen more
than 10 of my own friends lose their
virginity and then have their boyfriends
leave the next few days. Just trust in
God's love, because ~~His~~ love is eternal.

(Female, age 19)

Stay pure! Your husband will love
you that much more, and you'll be able
to love yourself. Don't ever think that
your body is something you can use
to make guys happy. Your husband is
going to love it no matter what.

(Female, age 16)

Staying pure is HARD, but it's worth it!
And God will bring you many blessings
to your marriage!

(Female, age 17)

From my personal experience, I would say to all the girls out there that we hold great power in our hands. We have the power to decide what kind of love we want to experience—the love of the world, or an unfailing love.

(Female, age 20)

After my own experiences with sex, I now understand that sex is meant to be something precious. Before marriage, sex is not the beautiful thing that God intended it to be. It only brings pain and heartbreak. I didn't want to listen to anyone's advice. I felt I had to make my own mistakes. But that was the most foolish decision I ever made. My healing process is going to be long and painful. God loves me more that any man ever will!

(Female, age 17)

Don't even start to play with fire!

(Male, age 15)

Don't do it. It's way cooler to stay pure!

(Male, age 20)

Do not give in to temptation. Stay pure until you get married. When you open that door, it's more than just losing your virginity. A lot of emotions come into play and you don't even know it or why.

(Female, age 18)

I wish someone had told me early on that it's good to be innocent. Don't be so curious about sex or the physical stuff.

(Female, age 17)

Realize that a "small" decision such as having sex can affect your whole life.

(Female, age 18)

Wait. Wait, even when you think you're ready. Wait.

(Female, age 15)

Waiting to have sex is truly worth it— not only to keep that gift, but also to keep your emotions clear.

(Female, age 19)

Save yourself for marriage. It is the greatest gift and token of love you can give to your future mate!

(Female, age 21)

Be yourself in God, and treat yourself like a princess because of our Lord. Save yourself for your husband.

(Female, age 21)

Tell your parents if you have made a mistake; they might be mad, but they will help you. Talk to people in your church, and don't hide anything. Get counseling within the church. I understand it's hard to understand, but God loves you no matter what you have done.

(Female, age 18)

Give our generation a good rep. We don't want to be known as the drunk, high, stupid and pregnant generation.

(Female, age 16)

DON'T DO IT! It really isn't worth it to have to deal with all the emotional baggage.

(Female, age 17)

You are valuable and worthy. Protect your purity and, if you lost it, know that the Lord can restore you and give you value and worth! In my own life, everything changed after I had sex with a guy and he didn't marry me. It's not worth it!

(Female, age 24)

Having sex before marriage is just not worth it. Waiting until marriage will save you a lot of heartbreak and scares and from getting diseases. I think life is simply better when you wait.

(Female, age 19)

Save your virginity.

(Female, age 16)

Emotional purity is just as important for girls as sexual purity! This needs to be taught FIRST. There would be no worry of sexual purity if our hearts were pure first. Instead, we end up with both problems.

(Female, age 19)

The biggest problem I've seen is that when young people get into a dating relationship, they think making out and cuddling is just normal. Not enough youth groups teach about courting. No one really understands it, so they date by the world's standards.

(Female, age 19)

Before you even get into a relationship, make sure you are totally satisfied and fulfilled and whole in your relationship with Jesus Christ—your true love!

(Female, age 19)

In today's society, it is extremely difficult to stay pure. The only way to stay pure is by trusting in God and putting your hope in Him. It is absolutely impossible to do it any other way! Trust God.

(Male, age 19)

Sex is awesome, but outside of marriage it will not reach its full potential. This is because sex isn't only a physical journey, but also an emotional high.

(Male, age 22)

Never be unequally yoked. The man should have strong
convictions, so don't waste your time dating
in middle school or high school. Be careful what you
watch on TV and don't kiss or do anything that will make
you stumble. Guard your heart!

(Female, age 22)

Satan's greatest tactic to get anyone to fall
is deceit. He will make it seem like sex is a good
thing to do even if you are not married.
The world's view on love is so misguided, but
God's definition is the truest. He created it.
The Lord is your bridegroom. Fall in love with
Jesus Christ first and stay in His Word.

(Female, age 19)

As we conclude this book, I encourage you right now to make some decisions about your future. If you want to have the greatest sex life in the history of humankind, there are two things you need to do:

1. *Commit to living with absolute purity.* On page 183 is a certificate you can sign in which you state that you are going to guard your eyes, your heart and your

body from anything that is impure. You do not have to let the world tell you what sex is all about.

2. *Be accountable to others.* The second form is one you can use to commit to live with purity once you begin a dating relationship. Have your parents, your youth pastor or your friends sign it—anyone whom you don't mind getting into your face if they see you start to slip. In fact, I would encourage you to have them periodically ask you, "Hey, you guys are keeping it pure, aren't you? You're not having sex, are you?" In this way, it will become a regular part of your purity discussion.

Keeping your mind and your body pure for your future spouse will set you up for the most incredible ecstasy that you could ever dream of. Remember that God invented sex, and He is the only one who can ensure that you get that ecstasy. Whatever you do, do it God's way!

Purity Commitment Form

I have made a covenant with my eyes . . .

Job 31:1

Because I want to honor God and love Him wholeheartedly, I commit to God, my family, and my (future) children to maintain and live by the highest biblical standard of purity in this generation.

Therefore, I commit . . .

1. To refuse participation in any conversations that promote or joke about immorality.

2. To confess to the same trusted friend each time I view pornography or have any sexual contact outside of marriage.

3. To register with technology that promotes the wisdom and safety of technology whether or not I struggle with pornography.

4. To show the fruit of repentance that, if I should stumble, I will go with my trusted friend and confess my sin to a leader in my life.

5. (For accountability friend): To hold any confession of failure in sexual immorality in strict confidence.

6. (For accountability friend): To share with leadership if my friend repeatedly stumbles in immorality.

7. (For leaders): To follow the process of bringing those who continue in immorality to the appropriate level of "discipline" instead of offering unsanctified "mercy."

Signed,

_____   _____

[name]   [date]

Source: http://www.ihop.org/Groups/1000033221/International_House_of/Old_Pages/
About_IHOP_KC/Purity_Covenant/Purity_Covenant.aspx.

Accountability Commitment Form

In pursuit of purity and Christlikeness, _____ and _____ make an open declaration to uphold a principled and disciplined standard of affection during our dating relationship. We have prayed, sought council from mentors, received approval from our spiritual covering and believe the following standards are honorable, wise and most importantly pleasing to the Lord.

We are, in a disciplined manner, available to lean on each other, put our arms around each other, place our head on each other's shoulder, rest our heads together and walk arm in arm. We choose not to allow faces to touch each other, hold hands, or allow personal areas to make contact in any way during our courtship.

In addition, we will never:

- Be alone in a building together
- Be alone in a vehicle after sundown
- Be in each other's dwellings after 10 PM unless a group is present
- Be alone past midnight

We not only commit to uphold these written standards during our courtship but also agree to discontinue any written or unwritten activity if we recognize impurity or selfishness arising within us.

Signed,

_____   _____
[name]   [date]

_____   _____
[name]   [date]

Endnotes

Chapter 1: Friends with So-called "Benefits"

1. Ana Dragovic, "Teen Vogue survey reveals teens' views on 'hooking up,'" *Teen Vogue*, May 2009. http://www.teenvogue.com/connect/blogs/soundoff/2009/05/teen-vogue-survey-reveals-teens-views-on-hooking-up.html (accessed January 2010).

Chapter 3: What Our Culture Says About Sex

1. Carlos McKinney and Youngdell Nash, "Bed," © Warner Brothers Music Corporation, Los Angeles, California.

2. Charles Brown, Cornell Haynes and Pharrell Williams, "Hot in Here," © Universal Music/MGB Songs, Beverly Hills, California.

3. Bryan Abrams, Mark Calderon, James Clarke, "I Wanna Sex You Up," © EMI Music, New York, New York.

4. Ellis Garrett, Eric Seats and Rapture Stewart, "Rock the Boat," © Black Fountain Music, c/o EMI Music, New York, New York.

5. Eric Hudson, Kawn Prather, John Stephens and Jessyca Wilson, "P.D.A. (We Just Don't Care)," © Ghetto Street Funk Music, c/o Music of Windswept, Los Angeles, California.

6. R. Kelly, "Ignition," © Jive Label Group, New York, New York.

7. Christopher Bridges, Melissa Elliott, Timothy Mosley and David Pomeranz, "One Minute Man," © EMI Music, New York, New York.

8. Anton Alexander, Youngdell Nash and Christopher Stewart, "This Ain't Sex," © Warner Brothers Music Corporation, Los Angeles, California.

9. Douglas A. Gentile, PhD, "Teen-Oriented Radio and Sexual Content Analysis," National Institute on Media and the Family, July 15, 1999. http://www.mediafamily.org/research/report_radiocontentanalysis.pdf.

10. The National Coalition for the Protection of Children and Families states that more shows are including sex-related scenes more often. In 1998, 67 percent of prime-time shows had sexual talk or behavior; in 2002 it increased to 71 percent; in 2005, to 77 percent. Among shows with sexual content, 5 scenes are shown per hour overall, 5.9 scenes are shown in primetime per hour, and 6.7 scenes are shown in teen shows per hour. "Sex and TV," Kaiser Family Foundation, *USA Today*, 2005.

11. Casey Williams, "MTV Smut Peddlers: Targeting Kids with Sex, Drugs and Alcohol," Parents Television Council, March 20, 2004. In 171 hours of MTV programming, PTC analysts found 1,548 sexual scenes containing 3,056 depictions of sex or various forms of nudity and 2,881 verbal sexual references. http://www.parentstv.org/PTC/publications/reports/mtv2005/main.asp.

12. "RAND Study Finds Adolescents Who Watch a Lot of TV with Sexual Content Have Sex Sooner," RAND Corporation, September 7, 2004. http://www.rand.org/news/press.04/09.07.html.

13. "Dirty Song Lyrics Can Prompt Early Teen Sex: Degrading Messages Influence Sexual Behavior, Study Finds," Associated Press, August 7, 2006. http://www.msnbc.msn.com/id/14227775/.

14. "Sexual Song Lyrics Linked to Early Sex," United Press International, February 24, 2009. http://www.upi.com/Health_News/2009/02/24/Sexual-song-lyrics-linked-to-early-sex/UPI-82341235457952/

15. Christine Lagorio, "Media May Prompt Teen Sex: Teens Exposed to the Most Sexy Media Images More Likely to Have Sex," CBS News, April 3, 2006. http://www.cbsnews.com/stories/2006/04/03/health/webmd/main1464262.shtml.

16. "Study Claims Sex on Television Contributes to Teen Pregnancy: New Study Reveals That Sexual Content on Television May Play a Role in Increased Rates of Teen Pregnancy," Buzzle, November 3, 2008. http://www.buzzle.com/articles/study-claims-sex-on-television-contributes-to-teen-pregnancy.html.

17. "Sex Thing," The Age, August 19, 2005. http://www.theage.com.au/news/music/sex-thing/2005/08/18/1123958136471.html.

18. "Shia LaBeouf on Seeing His Parents Having Sex and Smoking Pot," *Star* Magazine, June 10, 2009. http://www.starmagazine.com/shia_labeouf_interview_pots_sex/news/15696\.

19. Jem Aswad and Jennifer Vineyard, "Pink Speaks Out About Split With Carey Hart: 'We Love Each Other So So Much,'" MTV News, February 20, 2008. http://www.mtv.com/news/articles/1581962/20080220/pink.jhtml.

20. Kitty Raymond, "Scoop: Lindsay's Drama Dooms Sam Reunion," *San Francisco Examiner,* June 18, 2009. http://www.sfexaminer.com/entertainment/48317687.html.

21. "Marilyn Manson," Wikipedia, http://en.wikipedia.org/wiki/Marilyn_Manson; Kimberly Cutter, "Educating Dita," *Telegraph,* April 22, 2007. http://www.telegraph.co.uk/fashion/stellamagazine/3359949/Educating-Dita.html.

22. "Pam Anderson Files for Divorce," TMZ, November 27, 2006. http://www.tmz.com/2006/11/27/pam-anderson-files-for-divorce/.

23. Mary Margaret, "Rachel Bilson and Adam Brody Split," *People*, December 5, 2006. http://www.people.com/people/article/0,,1566162,00.html.

24. "Reese Witherspoon and Ryan Phillippe Split," *People*, October 30, 2006. http://www.people.com/people/article/0,,1552282,00.html.

25. "Usher Speaks Out for First Time Since Filing Divorce," *Insider,* http://www.theinsider.com/news/2289417_Usher_Speaks_Out_for_First_Time_Since_Filing_for_Divorce.

26. "Adolescent Sexuality in the United States: Sexuality in the Media," Wikipedia.org, citing "Teen Health and the Media," University of Washington Experimental Education Unit.

27. This has been well documented in shows such as PBS's *Frontline* program "The Merchants of Cool." http://www.pbs.org/wgbh/pages/frontline/shows/cool/.

Chapter 4: What Ignorant People Say About Sex

1. "Key Statistics from the National Survey of Family Growth," Centers for Disease Control and Prevention, cited in William Mosher, PhD, Anjani Chandra, PhD, and

Jo Jones, PhD, "Sexual Behavior and Selected Health Measures: Men and Women 15-44 Years of Age, United States, 2002," *Advance Data*, no. 362, September 15, 2005. http://www.cdc.gov/nchs/nsfg/abc_list_s.htm.

2. Jamie VanGeest, "Boynton Says Students Unaware of Oral Sex Dangers," *Minnesota Daily*, October 21, 2005, p. 1.

3. "Barriers During Oral Sex: The Wise Choice," Sex Info, November 13, 2008. http://www.soc.ucsb.edu/sexinfo/article/barriers-during-oral-sex-the-wise-choice.

4. "Men Look Away: Oral Sex REALLY Does Cause Some Throat Cancers," MailOnline: Science and Tech, April 8, 2009.

5. Ibid.

6. "Male Condoms: A Guide for Teens," Center for Young Women's Health, Children's Hospital Boston, 2009. http://www.youngwomenshealth.org/malecontraceptives1.html.

7. "How Effective Are Condoms?" Reality Check, 2008. http://www.realitycheckla.org/faqs/index.htm.

8. "Physicians Series Brochure: STDs," Physicians for Life, 2007. http://www.physiciansforlife.org/content/view/200/37/.

9. Yvette C. Cantu and Heather E. Farish, "The Human Papillomavirus (HPV) Epidemic: Condoms Don't Work," Family Research Council. http://www.ccv.org/downloads/pdf/HPV-Epidemic.PDF.

10. Dr. and Mrs. J.C. Willke, "Why We Can't Love Them Both," AbortionFacts.Com, 2006. http://www.abortionfacts.com/online_books/love_them_both/why_cant_we_love_them_both_35.asp.

11. http://www.avert.org/first-time-sex-stories.htm.

Chapter 5: What Kids Say About Sex

1. http://lovethosekids.com/moments/whatsex.htm.

2. http://lovethosekids.com/moments/pregnant.htm.

3. http://lovethosekids.com/moments/sleeping.htm.

4. http://www.davesdaily.com/funpages/funny-kids.htm.

5. http://www.atforumz.com/showthread.php?t=251085&page=3.

6. Laurie Pawlik-Kienien, "Kids' Thoughts on Love," Suite1-1.com. http://psychology.suite101.com/article.cfm/kids_thoughts_on_love#ixzz0JkyW85QP&C.

7. "Things People Said: Kids' Ideas About Love," RinkWorks. http://rinkworks.com/said/kidlove.shtml.

8. Ibid.

9. Ibid.

10. Ibid.

11. Lowell D. Streiker, *An Encyclopedia of Humor* (Peabody, MA: Hendrickson Publishers, Inc., 1998), p. 66.

Chapter 6: What Animals Say About Sex

1. "Lion," Wikipedia.com. http://en.wikipedia.org/wiki/Lion#Reproduction_and_life_cycle.

2. Swarag, "Strange Mating Rituals," OneIndia. http://living.oneindia.in/kamasutra/spheres-of-life/mating-rituals.html.

3. Swarag, "Strange Mating Rituals," OneIndia. http://living.oneindia.in/kamasutra/spheres-of-life/mating-rituals.html.

4. http://www.datepad.com/articles/top-10-weird-animal-mating-habits/#ixzz0I2wLIwXz&C.

5. Swarag, "Strange Mating Rituals," OneIndia. http://living.oneindia.in/kamasutra/spheres-of-life/mating-rituals.html.

6. Ibid.

7. James Clothier, "Sea Lion Mates Himself to Death," *The Sun,* July 23, 2009. http://www.thesun.co.uk/sol/homepage/news/2548510/Sea-lion-mates-himself-to-death.html.

8. http://www.datepad.com/articles/top-10-weird-animal-mating-habits/#ixzz0I2wLIwXz&C.

9. Ibid.

10. http://en.wikipedia.org/wiki/Gal%C3%A1pagos_tortoise.

11. Swarag, "Strange Mating Rituals," OneIndia. http://living.oneindia.in/kamasutra/spheres-of-life/mating-rituals.html.

12. Ibid.

13. http://www.datepad.com/articles/top-10-weird-animal-mating-habits/#ixzz0I2wLIwXz&C.

Chapter 11: What Those Who Waited Say About Sex

1. Annie Barrett, "Parents Television Council: There's Not Enough Sex on TV! (Sort of)," PopWatch, Entertainment Weekly, August 7, 2008. http://popwatch.ew.com/popwatch/2008/08/want-to-see-mor.html. Data based on a four-week time period.

2. Ira Teinowitz, "TV Finds Married Sex Boring, PTC Says," TV Week. http://www.tvweek.com/news/2008/08/tv_finds_married_sex_boring_pt.php. Data based on a study conducted by the Parents Television Council from September 23 to October 22, 2007.

3. "Authors of *The Case for Marriage* Talk About Why Married People Are Happier, Healthier, and Better Off Financially," Minnesota Family Council. http://www.mfc.org/contents/article.cfm?id=300.

4. Ibid.

5. Mike McManus, "To: Those Threatened by Divorce," Marriage Savers, 2001. http://www.preventingdivorce.com/marriage_savers__to.htm.

6. "Authors of *The Case for Marriage* Talk About Why Married People Are Happier, Healthier, and Better Off Financially." http://www.mfc.org/contents/article.cfm?id=300.

7. Hara Estroff Marano, "Debunking the Marriage Myth: It Works for Women, Too," the *New York Times,* August 2, 1998. http://www.divorcereform.org/mel/amarrandhealth.html.

8. Ibid.

About the Author

RON LUCE is the president and founder of Teen Mania Ministries, a Christian youth organization that reaches millions of young people worldwide.

Raised in a broken home, Ron ran away at the age of 15 and became involved in drugs and alcohols before finding Jesus at the age of 16. The life-transforming impact of Christ inspired Ron to dedicate his life to reaching young people. After receiving a bachelor's degree in theology and psychology and a master's degree in counseling, Ron and his wife, Katie, started Teen Mania in 1986 with nothing more than a Chevy Citation. Their dream was to raise up an army of young people who would change the world.

As a part of Teen Mania, Ron rallies teens all over the United States in arenas and stadiums at events called Acquire the Fire, with more than 3 million attendees to date. In addition, the 472-acre headquarters in Garden Valley, Texas, hosts the main campus of the Honor Academy, an internship that trains high school graduates to be leaders with honor and integrity. The weekly international television program *Acquire the Fire* and web initiatives reach hundreds of thousands monthly. Teen Mania has sent more than 62,000 teens all over the world on summer missions trips with Global Expeditions. Ron has also appeared as a teen culture expert on CNN's *God's Warriors,* ABC's Nightline, NBC, *The Sean Hannity Show, The O'Reilly Factor, 700 Club* and Focus on the Family.

Ron has also written 30 books for teenagers and their parents, including one of his newest releases, *ReCreate: Building a Culture in Your Home Stronger than the Culture Deceiving Your Kids*, which empowers parents of this young generation to reclaim influence in the home and take back the hearts and minds of their children. The teen version, *ReCreate Your World*, co-written by his daughter Charity Luce, was released to aid young people in their pursuit of taking back that which the culture has robbed them of. Ron is also the author of *Connecting with God: A Teen Mania Devotional*, which was published to help teens in their daily connection with God.

Ron and Katie live in Garden Valley, Texas, with their son, Cameron, while their two daughters, Hannah and Charity, are off at college.

CONTACT RON AT THE FOLLOWING:

Teen Mania Ministries Headquarters
P.O. Box 2000
Garden Valley, TX 75771
1-800-299-TEEN
info@teenmania.org

or visit:

Teenmania.com
Acquirethefire.com
Globalexpeditions.com